W9-BMC-849

WARRIORS OF
THE LORD

WARRIORS OF THE LORD

THE MILITARY ORDERS OF CHRISTENDOM

MICHAEL WALSH

WILLIAM B. EERDMANS PUBLISHING COMPANY
GRAND RAPIDS, MICHIGAN/CAMBRIDGE, U.K.

For Clare

First published in 2003 in the United Kingdom by John Hunt Publishing Ltd.,
46A West Street, Alresford, Hants SO24 9AU, U.K.
Tel: +44 (0) 1962 736880 Fax: +44 (0) 1962 736881
E-mail: office@johnhunt-publishing.com
www.johnhunt-publishing.com

This North American edition first published 2003
by Wm B. Eerdmans Publishing Co.,
255 Jefferson Ave. SE., Grand Rapids, MI 49503/
P.O.Box 163, Cambridge CB3 9PU U.K.
www.eerdmans.com

Printed by Tien Wah Press, Singapore

Eerdmans ISBN 0-8028-2109-X

Designed by Ian Hughes
www.mousematdesign.com

Illustrations:
Pages 2, 6, 12, 20, 24, 48, 69, 71, 87, 98, 106, 108, 124, 129 © 2003 The British Library/Heritage Images
Pages 10, 80 © 2003 Corporation of London/Heritage Images
Page 16 © 2003 The British Museum/Heritage Images
Page 18 © 2003 The Museum of London/Heritage Images
Pages 11, 19, 25, 26, 28, 33, 44, 53, 56, 61, 72, 74, 75, 88, 97, 100, 104, 114, 140, 164, 170, 177 © David Alexander

Illustration opposite title page: Saladin lays siege to Jerusalem

Contents

1 The Church and War   7

2 The Adversary   35

3 Crusades   63

4 Defense of the Kingdom   86

5 Northern Frontier   113

6 Reconquista   132

7 Rule of Life   155

8 Aftermath   169

Appendix 1   187

Appendix 2   193

Bibliography   204

Chapter One

The Church and War

This is a book about monks who were also soldiers. They were not soldiers accidentally, thrown into battle because their monastery was attacked by marauders. Nor were they monks who had once been soldiers but then, disenchanted, as was not an uncommon happening in the Middle Ages, by the life of a warrior, by all the slaughter and the pillaging, exchanged their armor for a religious habit and a life bounded by the walls of an abbey and the three vows of poverty, chastity, and obedience. The monks of this story, the Knights Templar, the Knights Hospitallers of St John of Jerusalem, the Teutonic Knights and others, had all freely chosen to live a religious life which involved, as part of their Christian vocation, the obligation to go to war and, if need be, to kill their adversaries.

In the early Middle Ages the most evident form of religious life in both the Latin West and the Greek East would have been monastic, groups of men living together under a common set of regulations, the "rule". Historically, however, the first form of religious life to emerge, towards the end of the third century, was that of the hermit, men and women leaving their homes with all its social ties and going into the Egyptian desert to be alone with God. Why it appeared when it did is a matter of debate, but it may have something to do with the end of the persecution of Christianity, the life of a hermit as a new form of martyrdom, men and women sacrificing all to follow Christ.

Opposite: Siege warfare in the Middle Ages

This solitary (or "eremetical" as it is called) form of life soon developed into something rather different. The hermits gravitated to people who were thought to be particularly good guides to the spiritual life – to "gurus" as they might be called in another faith tradition. They began to live in communities, and so the monastic (or "coenobitic") tradition emerged. But for people to live in this way there had to be an agreed set of rules. The best known of these, and the most detailed, is that attributed to St Benedict, which was written in Italy about AD 540. It lays down instructions for the abbot about the administration of the monastery, as well as the structure of the prayer life and the working life of the monks under his charge. Benedict did not think it all up anew. He drew upon the rule of St Basil. Basil had been first a hermit and then a monk before becoming Bishop of Caesarea – now Kayseri in central Turkey – in AD 370. What is called his rule, which is still the most common form of monastic life in the Churches of the East, is a series of questions and answers about the religious life, first composed by Basil before becoming a bishop, but afterwards revised both by himself and by others. There was also a rule attributed to St Augustine, the bishop of Hippo who died in AD 430, drawn at least in part from one of his letters. It was, however, little used until the eleventh century when it was adopted by already existing groups of priests who chose to live a more regulated life according to the traditional vows but without becoming monks in monasteries.

A reconstruction of the Abbey of Cluny

It has been customary to call the monasteries that existed in the West in the early Middle Ages "Benedictine", but this is a misnomer. Each monastery, once it was fully established, was entirely independent, and each developed its own way of life, some with little or no reference to the rule of St Benedict. A change came with the foundation in 909 of the abbey of Cluny, near Mâcon in Burgundy. Cluny tried to return to a strict observance of the rule of St Benedict, with a particular emphasis on the saying of the "office", the recitation by the monks in common of the psalms with other prayers and readings, and of worship in general. Many other abbeys followed Cluny's lead. Though the monks of Cluny and of the other abbeys following Cluny's lead had a great deal of influence in the reform of the Church, the Cluniacs did not constitute a religious Order: individual monasteries were still independent of each other, at least at first. The first "Order" as such was the Cistercians, named from its first monastery, at Citeaux, just south of Dijon, in the year 1098. The Cistercians, to some extent in reaction to the Cluniacs, lived a very simple life, a simplicity that was reflected in the plainness of its churches, in the lack of ornamentation in the monasteries and in the vestments used at worship. There were strict rules about food, about the necessity of observing silence to create an atmosphere of prayer, and about manual work for the monks. Citeaux was a great success, and founded numerous "daughter houses", which in turn founded others. Eventually they came all to be governed by a general chapter, or council, of all the abbots of all the monasteries following the Cistercian rule, and what the general chapter decided was to be observed by all.

Among historians there is some dispute whether, after all, Cistercians can be called the first religious Order. The structure which bound together the abbeys was fairly late in developing, the argument runs, and before it came into being, another group had emerged which could, because of its strict hierarchical constitution, more accurately claim to be the first religious Order: the Knights Templar.

HOLY WARRIORS

The Cistercians still exist: the Templars, on the other hand, have entirely disappeared. They were suppressed in 1312 by Pope Clement V, leaving behind them a plethora of legends of their great wealth, of their occult practices, of their extraordinary, even magical, power. None of these stories are true though they have been, by some modern writers, much elaborated and exploited for profit. But the Templars, like the other military Orders, are still remembered, right across Europe and in the Middle East, through the ruins of great castles, smaller "commanderies", churches and other buildings. Another, rather odd, survival in London is their name attached to a couple

The Inner Temple in 1829

of the quasi colleges, still called "inns", where British lawyers are trained – the Temple, and the Inner Temple.

Unlike the Templars, the Knights Hospitallers, though better known now as the Knights of Malta for reasons to be explained later, has survived as a religious Order down to the present day. Even if the vast majority of its members no longer take the three vows, which traditionally define a Christian as a member of an Order, some of them still do so, about 40 or so. Their role, however, has changed. Or rather, from being organized for warfare, they have reverted to something more like what was intended when the Order first began.

The Knights Hospitallers started as a group of men dedicated to taking care of pilgrims visiting the Holy Places of Palestine – Bethlehem, where Jesus was born, Nazareth where he grew up, and especially Jerusalem, where he died, was buried and,

Opposite: The Church of the Nativity, Bethlehem

The Betrayal of Christ

as Christians believe, rose from the dead. Now the Knights of Malta have hospitals around the world – there is one in Bethlehem – as well as ambulance services, health centers and orphanages. The St John Ambulance Brigade, whose volunteers faithfully turn up at football matches and wherever large crowds gather for public events, is a Protestant offshoot of the Knights. It is a far cry from the time when the Knights battled on land and on sea to defend, and to advance, the boundaries of Christianity.

To a modern mind, that they did so at all seems odd. It is not usual to associate men of war with men of religion. There is always Friar Tuck, of course, the traditionally rotund clergyman who, according to legend, was a member of the band of well-meaning outlaws commanded by Robin Hood. The stories of Robin Hood are set in the last decade of the twelfth century. At that time, when the English King Richard I, Richard the Lionheart, was absent from the country either on crusade in the Holy Land or held for ransom by the Emperor Henry VI, it is doubtful whether there were any such things as friars at all. But as we have just seen, there were certainly monks, and of course many other clergy. The incongruity of Friar Tuck is that here is a man of God consorting with a gang of armed men. For a clergyman, such behavior, however well intentioned, seems distinctly odd. Christianity, after all, has had a long history of being opposed to warfare.

Just how opposed, however, is a matter of debate. Some modern-day Christian pacifists have argued that in the early Church military service was strictly forbidden. Certainly the teaching of Jesus seems to suggest something of the sort – he tells his disciples to "turn the other cheek" if slapped on one, rather than to retaliate. And when, in the Garden of Gethsemane, Jesus was about to be arrested, one of his followers – Peter – drew a sword, Jesus told him to put it back in its scabbard. Those who live by the sword, he warned, will die by it. "Every soldier of later times was ungirded by the Lord when he disarmed Peter," said Tertullian, a Christian theologian writing in Africa early in the third century.

Yet even Tertullian admits that by his time – he died c. AD 220 – Christians were already serving in the Roman army. He tells the story, apparently a true one, of the "Thundering Legion" which, in the year AD 173 was saved from almost certain destruction by a violent thunderstorm. This storm both replenished the Legion's

Origen of Alexandria

empty water barrels, and put its barbarian enemy to flight. Tertullian, and other Christian writers, attributed the thunderstorm to the prayers of Christian soldiers serving in the Legion. Pagan authors, on the other hand, suggest that it was thanks to the intercession of the Emperor Marcus Aurelius — or even, in another variation, of an Egyptian magician.

Origen, another Christian author, this time from Alexandria, was a slightly younger contemporary of Tertullian. He was adamant that Christians should not fight, arguing that prayers, if believers really got down to it, would be just as effective. He is not against fighting as such, acknowledging that there might be such a thing as a just war. But even so, Christians were to have no part of it.

But why not? One reason may be that service in the Roman army was not simply a military duty, but an all-embracing religious commitment as well. There was the cult of the standard, the eagle, which each Legion carried. There was the oath each soldier had to swear to the Emperor. There was a long list of religious observances, rather like the liturgical calendar of Christian churches, which legionaries had to observe. Some Christians found ways round all these pagan rituals, but other refused.

There is, for instance, the story of Maximilian, a 21-year-old, who was brought by his father to the proconsul of the province of Mauretania in Africa. Maximilian's father wanted him to sign on as a soldier, but the son refused. The story is reported more or less word for word and precisely dated — 25 March 295 — which suggests that it was written down by a secretary as it occurred, as were a number of accounts of the martyrdom of Christians. Dion, the proconsul, tried to persuade him to accept the army's seal around his neck by arguing that even in the bodyguard of the emperor there were Christians. "They know

The Emperor Diocletian

what is best for them," Maximilian answered, "but I am a Christian and cannot do something that is wrong." He was put to death.

Dion obviously knew that there were indeed Christian soldiers serving close to the Emperor Diocletian. A story is recorded of a pagan priest casting auspices in the Emperor's presence. The Christians who were nearby, to distance themselves from the pagan ceremony, made what was probably a sign of the cross on their foreheads. The auspices did not come out as required, and the priest blamed its failure on the action of the Christians. Diocletian was furious. He ordered everyone in his palace to offer sacrifice – which Christians could not do – and those who refused were to be scourged. He also ordered that all the troops in his armies should offer sacrifice, and if they would not do so they were to be dismissed. Soon afterwards, in 303, he ordered the most widespread and sustained persecution that Christianity had hitherto endured.

But if the official religious life of the troops was the only thing keeping Christians out of the army, then all should have changed when, in the second decade of the fourth century, Christianity was tolerated, and rapidly became the official religion of the Empire. Yet attitudes to military service did not change – at least, not entirely.

RULES

Sometime in the late fourth or early fifth century there was compiled a list of rules governing the Christian assembly for worship, known as the Canons of Hippolytus. Canon XIV, which is thought to date from the fourth decade of the fourth century, insists that:

(1) No Christian should voluntarily become a soldier.

(2) If he becomes a soldier he should not shed blood (which seems a rather peculiar provision for a soldier).

(3) If he does shed blood he should stay away from the "sacred mysteries" , should not attend church, in other words, until he has done penance – though what that penance might be is not defined.

And towards the end of the century popes laid down that no one who had become a soldier after receiving baptism, could later be ordained as a priest. The fact that two popes had to insist on this suggests that it had happened. It was also forbidden for any priest to serve in the army.

St Augustine in his study

It was the great St Augustine who on warfare, as on almost every other major theological issue, laid down the outline of a Christian theory, which others later elaborated upon. His thinking seems to have gone through three stages. In the first, soon after his conversion – although his mother Monica was a Christian he was not baptized until he was well over 30 years old – he simply regarded war as part of the natural, legal order of things. In the second stage, around the time he became a bishop of Hippo in the province of Numidia in Africa, which happened in 395, he looked upon warfare as a means by which God achieved his purpose in converting the pagans. Paganism had recently staged a comeback, supported by the military force of a would-be usurper of the imperial throne. The Emperor Theodosius, who had not hitherto always behaved impeccably in matters of religion, now acted swiftly and brutally to suppress the revolt. Augustine approved.

But then, in 410, the city of Rome fell to barbarians under the command of Alaric the Goth (though Alaric, it should be said, was a Roman general). The shockwaves of this disaster spread to all parts of the Empire, and especially to Africa, where many Roman refugees fled for safety. The fall of Rome inspired Augustine to write perhaps his greatest book, *On the City of God*. In it he looks upon war with surprising equanimity. Everyone, he says, has to die sometime. What is wrong with war, therefore, is not so much the killing as the lust for domination (to which, he says, Rome itself had been prey), and the savagery and cruelty of it all. War is just, he says, if it is declared by a competent authority after due consultation and, he seems to say, if it is fought for defensive purposes.

And then he adds something rather odd, but which no doubt came as a consolation to soldiers. Whatever they do in warfare, he says, provided they are obeying the orders of their legitimate superiors, is itself justified. They do not have to question the morality of the orders they have been given. (Though to be fair to him, he says elsewhere that one must not obey a law — and therefore presumably a command — which one knows to be unjust.)

Augustine had a good friend who was a soldier, Boniface, the General in command of the province of Numidia. The General's wife died, and in his distress Boniface wrote to Augustine to say that he was thinking of giving up his military career and becoming a monk. Augustine, who quite possibly did not believe in the sincerity of the General's new-found vocation, wrote back persuading him of the value of the life of a soldier. To do so, he drew a comparison with the life of a monk. The soldier, he pointed out, fights against the monk's enemies, but the monk for his part fights the soldier's enemies — not barbarian warriors but demons. The monk, Augustine adds, practices poverty, chastity and obedience — but the soldier must practice chastity within marriage, and he must keep his desires in check or he will be overcome by avarice. A soldier's skill must be dedicated to the service of God's people, and the peace he brings through warfare will be a foreshadowing of that heavenly peace for which all Christians strive. By a curious turn of fate in 430 Boniface, who had in the interim singularly failed to live up to the ideal put before him in that letter, was in charge of defending Hippo from the Vandals as Augustine lay dying inside the city.

Augustine, then, provided a rationale for a just war, one in which Christians could engage without betraying their faith. But the Church's innate hostility to the idea of warfare did not change for centuries. At least, that is, in the Western part. For the Empire was slowly but inexorably dividing into two.

Bronze head of Constantine I

BIRTH OF A CITY

In 313 the Emperor Constantine and his co-Emperor Licinius wrote a letter to provincial governors commanding freedom of worship for Christians, and the restitution of any of their goods that had been confiscated. Because Constantine and Licinius were meeting in Milan, the letter has been called the "Edict of Milan". Just over a decade later, when the conflict which had subsequently broken out between the two Emperors was resolved by Licinius' defeat, Constantine decided to build a new capital in the East of the Empire, one which would be a Christian city, unlike the ancient, and still largely pagan, city of Rome. The site he chose was the ancient Greek colony of Byzantium on the Bosphorus. It was renamed Constantinople, and celebrated its birthday as 11 May 330.

It was built to mirror Rome. There was a senate, made up of some Roman senators and others from provincial capitals. They — and other citizens — enjoyed privileges equivalent to those they would have been accorded in Rome. There were great buildings and new churches. Works of art were shipped from Italy, and saints' relics installed. It was even divided, like the old Rome, into fourteen regions. It is now

The Theodosius Obelisk, Istanbul, Turkey

known as Istanbul: just as the old Rome had been referred to simply as "the City", so the new Rome was also called "the City", though in Greek of course, rather than in Latin, and it is from the Greek for "the City" that its modern name is distantly derived.

At the end of the fourth century, when the Emperor Theodosius died, his two sons divided the Empire out between them, the elder settling as Emperor in Constantinople. Less than a century later there was no longer a Roman Emperor ruling in the West. Instead the emperors were replaced by a succession of barbarian kings, frequently, from the Church's point of view, of doubtful orthodoxy.

In the East, however, the enemy was different – and much older. Under the Sassanid dynasty, Persia had once more emerged as a threat to the Roman Empire. Under Shapur I the fire worshipping Zoroastrian kings laid claim to all lands in Asia

The walls of Constantinople, Turkey

Minor under the power of Rome. That was in the third century. Roman emperors were defeated in battle; one, Valerian, was even more shamefully captured in 260. Just over a century later the Emperor Julian, the Apostate as he was called, the last pagan Emperor, was defeated and killed by Shapur II as he tried to restore Roman authority in the East. The Persian Empire stretched from the Oxus River in the North to the Indus River in the South, from China to Arabia to the Caspian Sea. It had established its Western borders on its frontier with Armenia, and so never quite reached the Mediterranean. Under Khusrau II, Khusrau the Victorious, that was to change.

Shapur displays a portrait of Khusrau to a visiting dignitary

Khusrau had begun his reign in 590 as anything but victorious. He had been put on the throne in Ctesiphon, the Persian capital, by a rebellious general, but then driven out. He appealed to the Emperor Maurice in Constantinople for help, which was given, and successfully: Khusrau was restored, and for the rest of Maurice's reign relations between the two powers were friendly. Unhappily for Maurice, however, in 602 his army mutinied. He had in his turn to appeal for help to the Persian king, but he and his sons were killed before an answer arrived.

Khusrau was furious that he had not been able to save his old ally. He launched an assault against the usurper in Constantinople, and his campaign met little resistance from a Byzantine army already weakened by the civil war and its aftermath. In 614 the Persian armies reached the Byzantine territories bordering the Mediterranean, capturing Syria, Damascus falling without resistance. As the Persian army advanced it was joined by the Jews of the area, eager to take revenge on the Christians who had oppressed them. Monasteries and convents were devastated. The Patriarch of Jerusalem negotiated a peaceful hand-over of the city to a Persian garrison, but there was a revolt inside the walls, some of the Persian garrison, and some of the Jews who had accompanied them, were slaughtered in the uprising. The Persian commander returned, spurred on, it was said, by the Zoroastrian priests who represented King Khusrau, and by Jews seeking vengeance.

What happened next was vividly described by a local monk, Antiochus Strategos, who survived the massacre. His account leaves little to the imagination:

> The evil foemen entered the city in great fury, like infuriated wild beasts and irritated serpents. The men, however, who defended the city wall, fled and hid themselves in caverns, fosses and cisterns in order to save themselves; and the people in crowds fled into churches and altars; and there they destroyed them. For the enemy entered in mighty wrath, gnashing their teeth in violent fury; like evil beasts they roared, bellowed like lions, hissed like ferocious serpents, and slew all whom they found. Like mad dogs they tore with their teeth the flesh of the faithful, and respected none at all, neither child nor baby, neither priest nor monk, neither virgin nor widow. [1]

It was one of the greatest massacres in history.

There was, however, worse to come. In 326 the Empress Helena, Constantine's mother, on a pilgrimage to Jerusalem had found what she, and the Church of

Jerusalem, believed to be the very cross upon which Jesus had been crucified. It became Jerusalem's, and the Church's, most precious relic, and was hidden for safety during the attack. Now in a garden near the Patriarch's palace the Persians unearthed a box containing

The Empress Helena and the Cross of Christ

the remains of the cross. The Patriarch, who had been tortured to reveal its whereabouts, accompanied it into exile as it was sent to the court of King Khusrau as a present to his Christian wife. And, as a final humiliation to the Christians, the administration of Jerusalem was once again put into the hands of the Jews.

This last provision did not long endure. Many of the Christians who had suffered under the Persians as they advanced through Syria were themselves at odds with the regime in Constantinople and were therefore natural allies of the Persians. Moreover, Khusrau had set his sights on capturing the Christian land of Egypt: his army's treatment of Christians in Syria would make conquest of that country more difficult, the Egyptians more determined to resist. In 617, therefore, Christians were once again given control of Jerusalem, and the Jews once again exiled.

But in Constantinople the Emperor Heraclius had been humiliated. Not only had the most precious symbol of Christianity been seized by fire worshippers, by 620 Egypt had fallen and the supply of grain to feed Constantinople had been cut off. Heraclius had to respond or the Roman Empire in the East would be at an end. In 620 he began to prepare for a holy war.

The Emperor Heraclius in his tent and Chosroes, King of Persia

The problem for the Emperor was that his defeated army was both exhausted and demoralized. He had to start again to build it up, and to do so he needed money. His own treasury was empty, but the Church was still wealthy. The Patriarch Sergius of Constantinople backed Heraclius as he had done ever since his triumphant accession to power in 610. He ordered that golden ornaments and plates, anything of value that was not of immediate necessity in the divine liturgy, be melted down and handed over for the support of the army. The Emperor minted new coins. On one side were the Emperor and his son, on the other the cross. Each coin proclaimed, "God has chosen the Romans."

But Heraclius was careful. He took time to launch his campaign, and even when he did so he knew that the Persian army outnumbered his, and was more skilled in battle. He told his troops to put their trust in God. "When God wills it," he said to them, "one man will rout a thousand. So let us sacrifice ourselves to God for the salvation of our brothers. May we win the crown of martyrdom that we may be praised in future and receive our recompense from God." [2]

That this was a holy war, that his soldiers, should they die in battle, would be commemorated as martyrs because they were fighting for a Christian cause, was something new in Christian rhetoric, and it was repeated by Heraclius time and again. He had adopted this language as his own before it was taken up by Muhammad with his concept of the jihad (cf. the next chapter). Ultimately Heraclius triumphed over the fire-worshipping Persians, having appealed for support to those Christians within the Persian Empire whose beliefs divided them from the orthodoxy of Constantinople, but who had been shocked by the seizure of the Holy Cross. Although in the course of the war against Khusrau the Persian army, backed by their barbarian allies the Avars, reached the walls of Constantinople, Heraclius eventually triumphed. In December 627 the Persian army was completely overwhelmed by a day-long battle at Nineveh; by the end of the year the nearby Persian capital Ctesiphon had been taken. Though the campaign dragged on, there was no longer doubt about the outcome. The True Cross, however, took some finding. Finally, in 630, walking into the city as a pilgrim, Heraclius carried the relic back to Jerusalem. The feast, which is called the Exaltation of the Holy Cross, celebrated by Christians on 14 September, commemorates the event. It turned out to be a hollow victory. A new holy war was about to be engaged, one that would again take administration of the holy sites of Jerusalem out of the hands of Christians. The story will be told in the chapter that follows.

In the East, then, warfare had taken on a religious significance. In the West, on the other hand, the old clerical disdain for war and for warriors continued to hold sway. There were, no doubt, many reasons for this. The Empire fragmented. There were many kings of barbarian ancestry, many, if not most, of them holding heretical views. But at least they were Christian, so the issue of a holy war, as war against the infidel, did not arise. There was even a handful of Christian writers who, in the late sixth and early seventh century, appeared to praise military virtue. They did so at least in part because they saw the new barbarian overlords as the only hope for establishing firm government in the West, something the Emperor Heraclius seemed incapable of doing.

But, as the centuries went by, peace seemed no closer. Charlemagne established a degree of unity, but it was beyond the power of his successors to maintain it. The conflicts they engaged in were the struggles of petty warlords, little touching the lives of most – except in the devastation of the countryside that accompanied their military enterprises. It must have seemed, in tenth-century France, that the world had descended into anarchy. The trouble was two-fold: the emergence of a warrior class, and the growing power of castles and those who dwelt in them.

THE WARRIOR CLASS

It was from the warrior class that knights (the Anglo-Saxon word from which "knight" is derived means "servant") such as the Hospitallers and Templars emerged. When the English King Alfred, who died at the very end of the ninth century, was translating into Anglo-Saxon *On the Consolation of Philosophy* by the Roman philosopher Boethius, he distinguished three classes in society: there were those who worked the field, he said,

and those who prayed – the monks, nuns and priests – and there were knights who fought to safeguard the others. These were, fundamentally, heavily armored mounted soldiers. The armor they wore developed over time from leather to chain mail to full plate armor – this last only by the mid-fifteenth century – but it was always expensive, which meant that knights had to be relatively wealthy. Indeed, in some parts of Europe where horses were fairly plentiful simply a helmet itself might cost as much as a knight's mount. To be able to afford to buy the equipment for himself and for

King Alfred the Great on his throne

his horse a knight had to belong to a landowning family.

Landowning was central to another aspect of knighthood: the loyalty owed by knights to their lords. In the feudal system land was commonly held by a family in return for a form of service to the person, their lord, to whom the land formally belonged. This was the system of vassalage, and the lord to whom a lesser noble swore loyalty in return for his lands was his liege lord – except in England where liege loyalty was sworn only to the king. Underlying this notion was the memory of the loyalty that a German warrior had owed to his leader but it became complicated because it was perfectly possible for one nobleman to hold lands of several others, to each of whom he, theoretically at least, owed service. If his various lords happened to be at odds with one another, this presented a problem – hence the swearing of fealty to a "liege" lord, who (again in theory because it become not uncommon to have

Image of kneeling knight from Wittenberg, Germany

more than one liege lord) took precedence.

Knights, then, were mounted, armored warriors with some standing in society. They were at first not a clearly defined class, but the class began to be more closely defined as time went by, so that someone could only be born into it. Increasingly the rank and title was restricted to the sons of knights – possibly to keep down the numbers – and sons were formally made knights on reaching adulthood. The first records of men being "made knights" or being "dubbed" come from the last part of the eleventh century. The ceremony of "dubbing" seems to have involved being struck by a sword (as the ceremony is still performed today) or being buffeted by a fist, and then given the

A knight in armor

accoutrements of knighthood. In particular a sword was handed over, it having been first blessed by the Church. There was a strongly religious element in the making of new knights, starting with the bath, which was regarded as a form of spiritual, as well as bodily, purification, and ending with a vigil before an altar upon which a knight's sword lay. It seems clear that it was perfectly possible for a senior ecclesiastic to create knights – if only from evidence of people trying to ban such a practice.

Not only was the Church able to create knights, at least in the earlier days, it also tried to constrain them. The distinguishing feature of knights – because all soldiers fought on foot with a sword when need be – was that they charged into battle with a lance in the "couched" position. Tournaments, so closely associated with the romantic picture of "knights in armor" first seem to have emerged in Northern France at the end of the eleventh century as a means of turning a training exercise into a sport. But it was a dangerous sport. Even in serious combat knights did not usually kill each other. Though they may have slain ordinary foot soldiers they respected the rank of knightly adversaries and usually spared their lives. It was, in any case, more financially rewarding to ransom the defeated knight, and carry off his armor and his warhorse as booty. However, in tournaments, which were intended as entertainment though with a serious purpose, knights frequently got killed. Such deaths were accidental, but the Church was hostile to tournaments nonetheless because of the shedding of blood that sometimes occurred. In 1130 they were formally banned at the Council of Clermont.

> We entirely forbid, moreover, those abominable jousts and tournaments in which knights come together by agreement and rashly engage in showing off their physical prowess and daring, and which often result in human deaths and danger to souls. If any of them dies on these occasions, although penance and viaticum [i.e., the Eucharist] are not to be denied him when he requests them, he is to be deprived of a church burial

declared canon 14, and the penultimate canon, number 29, added

> We prohibit under anathema [i.e., excommunication] that murderous art of crossbowmen and archers, which is hateful to God, to be employed against Christians and Catholics from now on.

Archers, and especially crossbowmen, wreaked destruction on foot soldiers and knights alike, without consideration of social class. The knights who, in their armor, were normally relatively safe except from the assault of their own class, were at the mercy of arrows and crossbow darts fired by common soldiery who sometimes were — especially the crossbowmen — mercenary troops.

But there were two further canons of Clermont, numbers 11 and 12, that bore upon the lives of knights perhaps even more closely. They were, it seems, intended to protect the peasantry and the small but emerging middle class of merchants:

> We prescribe that priests, clerics, monks, pilgrims, merchants and peasants, in their coming and going and their work on the land, and the animals with which they plough and carry seeds to the fields, and their sheep, be left in peace at all times.

The castle of Tarascon overlooks the river Rhone in France

We decree that the truce is to be inviolably observed by all from sunset on
Wednesday until sunrise on Monday, and from Advent until the octave [i.e., eight
days after] of the Epiphany, and from Qinquagesima until the octave of Easter.
If anyone tries to break the truce, and does not comply after a third warning, let
his bishop pronounce sentence of excommunication on him . . .

To understand the background to these severe penalties imposed by the Church on
anyone fighting in the proscribed periods, which taken together covered about half the
year, it is necessary to go back to that other factor in the growth of violence in the
eleventh century, the growing significance of castles.

LANDS AND POSSESSIONS

Not that castles were a new phenomenon in the countryside, but their presence made
an already unstable situation increasingly unsafe. Possession of them enhanced the
prestige of the nobility, and there was a struggle to control them. Those whom the
noble put in charge of the castles which belonged to them – the castellans – frequently
became warlords in their own right, terrorizing the countryside, imposing their will on
the peasantry adjacent to the castle walls, and competing for resources of food and
water with other nearby garrisons. Moreover, in order to keep dynastic control over the
castles, the families who had obtained them were forced to change the system of
inheritance to primogeniture, so that only a single son inherited his father's property.
This in itself added to the number of dispossessed sons who were forced to seek other
means of support – often as members of the warrior class we now call knights.

Of particular concern to the Church was the regular appropriation of Church
lands, together with the pillaging of its valuables and even, apparently, the occasional
seizing of the relics of saints. Such was the instability, the chaotic violence unleashed
by the castellans' raiding parties and the petty wars between minor noblemen, that
churchmen determined to do something about restraining the destruction that was
being wreaked on the countryside. The movement came to the called "The peace (or
sometimes the truce) of God".

This movement began in the last couple of decades of the tenth century, backed both by senior churchmen – bishops and abbots – and by the higher nobility, the dukes and counts, whose lands were being appropriated by the unruly castellans. But above all, it was a popular movement, with great crowds attending the peace assemblies to view the relics of saints that had been gathered together for the occasion from the various shrines in the regions, and to swear on the relics to maintain peace.

The movement began in Southern France, and the first known assembly is that of Charroux in 989. Its decrees are remarkably similar to those quoted above from the Council of Clermont nearly a century and a half later. They were as follows:

> Following the example of my predecessors, I, Gunbald, archbishop of Bordeaux, called together the bishops of my diocese in a synod at Charroux . . . and we, assembled there in the name of God, made the following decrees:
>
> I. Anathema against those who break into churches. If anyone breaks into or robs a church, he shall be anathema unless he makes satisfaction.
>
> 2. Anathema against those who rob the poor. If anyone robs a peasant or any

Robert II, King of France, known as 'the Pious'

other poor person of a sheep, ox, ass, cow, goat, or pig, he shall be anathema unless he makes satisfaction.

3. Anathema against those who injure clergymen. If anyone attacks, seizes, or beats a priest, deacon, or any other clergyman, who is not bearing arms (shield, sword, coat of mail, or helmet), but is going along peacefully or staying in the house, the sacrilegious person shall be excommunicated and cut off from the church, unless he makes satisfaction, or unless the bishop discovers that the clergyman brought it upon himself by his own fault. [3]

Other dioceses of Southern France followed suit in the next few years. The assemblies were often occasions of religious revivalism as well as oath-swearing to keep the peace.

From the early years of the eleventh century the movement moved north, and was taken up by the French king, Robert the Pious. He swore not to seize a horse or mule from the beginning of March until the end of October, except to recover a debt, and from Lent to the end of the Easter season not to attack an unarmed knight – armed knights, presumably, were fair game. He also undertook not to attack noblewomen or nuns "unless it is their fault". His successor showed little interest in the movement, however, and the initiative again moved southwards, sparked perhaps by a prolonged period of famine which was seen by many as punishment from on high for their sins. So again the peace movement was linked to religious revivalism. This time it was often associated, on a local level, with the establishment of associations of the laity sworn to uphold the peace – and even if need be to go to war to do so.

In the 1020s the peace movement developed from an attempt to safeguard non-combatants from the depredations of warriors, to being a systematic effort to lay down periods during which there should be no fighting – which is the significant distinction between decrees of Charroux in 989 and those of the Council of Clermont, quoted above, not quite a century and a half later. In 1027 the Council of Elne laid down, in addition to the usual provisions for safeguarding clerics, women and peasants, that no one should attack his enemy from Saturday night to Monday morning: there was, in other words, to be no fighting on the holy day of Sunday which, in ecclesiastical terms, began on Saturday evening.

The best-known formulation of what had by now come to be known as "the Truce of God", in addition to the "peace", was drawn up in 1054 in the 29 decrees of the Council of Narbonne. A similar program was adopted two years later in Barcelona. For the movement was becoming international. It first extended outside France to Flanders. In 1041 the abbot of the great monastery of Cluny, Odilo, together with several of the bishops of southern France, sent a letter to the clergy of Italy urging them to adopt the Truce of God. That Abbot Odilo was involved was important. Cluny was closely associated with the eleventh-century reform of the Church. The Cluniac abbeys were scattered across Europe, and it may very well have been the influence of Cluny's abbot which gave impetus to the spread of the peace movement both inside and, especially, outside France – to Italy, Spain and Germany.

One of the most enthusiastic, and systematic, supporters of the Truce of God was Duke William of Normandy, England's William the Conqueror, who introduced a procedure into all parishes for the enforcement of the oaths that had been struck. This structure, which, as has been seen, was tried elsewhere, appears to have been particularly successful in Normandy, creating in William's home territory a relatively stable milieu from which, in 1066, he was able to launch his invasion of England.

Though the Church was not wholly opposed to war – and a remarkable

Pope Urban gives his blessing to the departing Crusaders

Opposite: The Abbey of Cluny, France

number of clerics are indeed known to have taken part in battles, despite the prohibition on clergy shedding blood – in the late tenth, and throughout the eleventh, century it was deeply involved in the movement to restrain violence in Christendom. The story was not quite as straightforward as that, which chapter 3 will recount, but the claim remains largely true. In such a context it seems surprising that, early in the twelfth century there should have emerged warrior monks such as the Hospitallers and Templars, who looked upon it as their Christian vocation to do battle on behalf of the Church.

A beginning of an explanation may be found in the Narbonne Peace Council of 1054. It had become common in such gatherings to list the groups of people who were, or ought to have been, immune from attack. Narbonne went further. It laid down the principle that to kill a Christian was to shed the blood of Christ, and no member of the Church would wish to do that. But what of the blood of those who were not Christians? When, at the end of the eleventh century, Pope Urban II called upon Christians – he was addressing the French in particular – to go on crusade, he put his plea within the context of the Truce of God. According to the Truce, they had undertaken not to wage war, at least for much of the year, upon their fellow countrymen and Christians. But the warlike tendencies of the warrior class, the knights, were not assuaged. Another enemy had to be found if they were not to return to shedding Christian blood.

Who that enemy was to be is the subject of the next chapter.

---

1. Quoted in Peters, F. E., *Jerusalem* (Princeton NJ: Princeton University Press, 1985), pp. 170–171.

2. Quoted in Regan, G., *The First Crusader* (Stroud: Sutton Publishing, 2001), p. 78.

3. Quoted in Thatcher, O. J. and McNeal, E. H. (eds.), *A Source Book for Medieval History*, (New York: Scribners, 1905), p. 412.

Chapter Two

The Adversary

They came riding out of Arabia, some 10,000 horsemen, it was said, and perhaps twice that many foot soldiers. It was October 630, and they did not stay, returning home in December. That was in Muhammad's lifetime. Muhammad himself died two years later, on 8 June 632 and Abu Bakr, like Muhammad a member of the Quraysh tribe, the man who had led the prayers in Mecca during the Prophet's absence, was appointed to succeed him. He was the Caliph – the Arabic word Khafila means successor. His full title was "Successor of the Messenger of God".

It was Abu Bakr who began in earnest the expeditions outside Arabia into the southern part of Mesopotamia. His armies were not always successful, but under his leadership, or under that of Umar, the successor he appointed on his deathbed in 634, they won battles more often than not. Looking back on it, the Muslim armies came to regard their success as little short of miraculous, a tribute to their new faith. Certainly Islam had united hitherto warring tribes within Arabia to a degree that was extraordinary. But there were other, more prosaic reasons for their triumph.

As the first chapter related, for half a millennium two great empires, Rome and Persia, had fought for control of the Middle East, first one side gaining the ascendancy then the other. This constant warfare had weakened both the new Rome and the Persian kingdom. Though Constantinople was to withstand the onslaught of Islam until the thirteenth century – and the city itself until the middle of the fifteenth century when it fell to the Ottoman Turks, its territory was much reduced. Persia, on the other hand, after the arrival of Islam, was soon to disappear as an independent state.

The Emperor in Constantinople regarded himself as the defender of Christian orthodoxy. But in the East of the Empire, far more so than in the West, this was no easy task. Doctrinal disputes about the nature of Christ, how it was that he was both God and man, had been resolved by councils attended by many of the Eastern bishops and by some representatives of the Western ones. But conciliar formulations, though in theory representing a consensus of opinion, had ultimately failed to satisfy everyone. Separate Churches, holding diverse interpretations of the nature of Christ, had emerged which were hostile to the orthodoxy that the Emperor, for the most part, tried to impose. There were Copts and Jacobites, Maronites, Nestorians, and Melkites. "Melkite" means royalist. This Church's members were loyal to the orthodoxy as interpreted in Constantinople. Nestorian Christians, on the other hand, were bitter opponents of the Byzantine state.

As well as often being opposed to the imperial power in the capital city of the Eastern Empire, these different churches could be equally hostile to each other. More significantly, perhaps, just because very many were opposed to the attempts of the Byzantine Emperor to impose his own version of Christian doctrine, some Christians were quite ready to welcome their new overlords as a relief from interference from Constantinople. One striking example of collaboration is the family of John of Damascus. He was a theologian and saint, someone still highly revered by Christians both East and West, and the first to make a scholarly comparison between Christianity and Islam — naturally to the advantage of the former (he seems to have regarded Islam as a Christian heresy). He was born about 650 and lived to be 100 or thereabouts. When he was 50 he entered a monastery in Jerusalem, but before becoming a monk he had served as a high official at the court of the Caliph in Damascus. His father had done likewise and, further back still, in 635 his grandfather had negotiated the surrender of the city of Damascus to the Muslim army, effectively bringing to an end the rule of the Byzantines in Syria.

Christians, therefore, who might have opposed the Arab forces led by

Muhammad and his successors, were not united among themselves and did not at first see Islam as a threat. Some, like John of Damascus, thought of it as yet another version of Christianity. In any case, there were Christian Arabs, members of the Syriac Christian churches. Christianity was by the seventh century well established in Arabia, on the Persian Gulf, in Oman and Yemen and among the nomadic tribes along the fringes of the Arabian peninsular, and above all across the water in Ethiopia. Christians though they were, they might have been expected to be sympathetic to their new rulers, and to collaborate with them. In a world where religious diversity, even among Christians, was a commonplace, they might not, at least at first, have recognized in Islam a distinctive, new, and possibly hostile, form of religious belief. The Qu'ran had not been written down: there was as yet no sacred book competing with the Bible, and there were traces of both Christianity and Judaism in the Islamic faith. After all, when in the early years of his conversion to monotheism Muhammad knelt to pray he turned not towards Mecca but towards Jerusalem.

In Jerusalem, its Christian and Jewish inhabitants were not therefore particularly alarmed when their city fell to the soldiers of Islam, especially when Muslim occupation was not followed by the wholesale slaughter which 22 years earlier had marked the arrival of the Persians. They had been expecting Jerusalem to fall ever since, in August 636, the Byzantine army had been defeated at the Battle of Yarmuk, on the left bank of the River Jordan. When the Muslims arrived in Jerusalem it was, by the Christian calendar, 638. By Muslim reckoning it was year 17. Year one in the Islamic calendar was counted from the flight of Muhammad from Mecca to Medina.

Muhammad ibn Abd Allah was born in Mecca about the year 570. He was born after his father's death, which excluded him from his inheritance, and therefore from the circle of Mecca's rich and powerful. Mecca had become one of Arabia's most wealthy cities at least in part because it was a sacred sanctuary where fighting was forbidden and trade could take place in relative peace. Moreover, it lay across the trade routes up from India or Ethiopia via Yemen and on to Damascus and Constantinople and points west. It had remained as far as it could politically neutral, dealing even-handedly with the Byzantines on the one side and the Persians on the other. It traded with men of all faiths, whether Zoroastrians or the various forms of Christianity or followers of tribal gods.

Muhammad, like most of the citizens of Mecca, was a member of the Quraysh tribe, but within the Quraysh his own clan, the Hashim, was one of the less powerful. He worked as a steward to Khadija, a rich woman trader, looking after her merchandise, but when he was 25 they were married. Some time afterwards he began to receive visions. At first he thought they came directly from God, but later he decided that they had been communicated to him by the Angel Gabriel, acting as an intermediary, and that he was himself, like Gabriel, a messenger of God, or prophet, conveying God's teaching to the people. It is this series of visions that were put down in the Qu'ran, though that did not happen until the middle years of the seventh century and a quarter of a century after Muhammad's death. The earliest of the revelations were quite short, but became longer as time went by – for he continued to receive these messages throughout his life.

The Kaaba in Mecca

At first he kept silent about his visions, but about 610 began to tell his friends. The message was, fundamentally, a call to righteousness and to worship. While there was nothing unusual in this, one aspect of Muhammad's message crucially distinguished it from anything that had gone before. In the Western part of the Arabian peninsular Christianity had not penetrated. There the dominant form of religion was a traditional one, which embraced a multitude of gods. The cult center in Mecca was the cube-shaped building, the Kaaba, where were housed the deities worshiped by the different tribes. But in the teaching of Muhammad there was but one God. His faith, like that of Judaism and Christianity, was monotheistic. There was no God but Allah, and Muhammad was his prophet.

Obviously this was a threat to the worship of the deities in the Kaaba. It was a threat, moreover, to Muhammad's own clan, the Hashim, because they were guardians and stewards of the cult of the god Hubal, whose image was among those in the Kaaba. And because it was a threat to the religious status quo in Mecca, and thus to the holy place which had provided sanctuary for the traders, it was potentially a threat to the prosperity of the town. Muhammad was looked upon in his city as a troublemaker, seeking to promote his own religious views as a vehicle for social and political change.

But there was another type of threat. The development of Mecca as a major trading center had meant that the moral code of the nomadic tribes was no longer adequate for the new kind of entrepreneurial society which had only fairly recently, and rather quickly, emerged. Muhammad's faith, as well as imposing monotheism, also demanded from its adherents a charitable concern for the poor. All, Muhammad said, would on the last day be judged by God according to their generosity to the needy. Almsgiving, he taught, was a particular obligation upon the wealthy.

The Hashim may have been guardians of the god Hubal, but they were also one of the weaker and poorer clans in Mecca. To them, the moral code taught by the Prophet, who was a member of their own clan, was a great attraction. Muhammad's first converts were drawn, not surprisingly, from amongst those closest to him. But from the wealthier Quraysh there came first opposition, and then persecution. In 615 Muhammad urged some of his followers to flee Mecca for Aksum, the capital, in

Northern Ethiopia, of a Christian kingdom which was the dominant power in the south of Arabia. But for those of the first generation of Muslims who remained in Mecca the situation grew even more desperate after the death in 619 of Abu Talib, Muhammad's uncle and protector, who was head of the clan. He was succeeded by another uncle of Muhammad's, Abu Lahab, who was not at all sympathetic. The Prophet himself had to consider leaving his native city. He chose to go to Yathrib, some 125 miles north of Mecca, an oasis town with a large Jewish population. It may indeed have been the presence of the Jews that attracted him: here was a monotheistic religious group which might have been expected to be sympathetic to his message.

Before he would agree to go, Muhammad demanded that the people of Yathrib acknowledge him as the Prophet of Allah. In June 622, 75 elders came and made the required pledge. Muslims began to slip out of Mecca and make their way north. Almost all left, in what became known as the "Hijra", or "the severing". Muhammad himself was one of the last to go. He arrived in Yathrib towards the end of September 622. The town's name became Medina, meaning "the Prophet's city".

There then began a series of skirmishes between the merchants of Mecca and the Muslims in Medina — who were soon joined by many of the leading men of the city. At one battle in 624, Muslim sources reported, the heavily out-numbered followers of Muhammad defeated a powerful force from Mecca. This Muhammad's followers took as a sign that God was on their side. A year later almost to the day the Muslims were very badly mauled, Muhammad himself being among the wounded: to make up for the dead warriors Muslims were encouraged to take up to four wives.

Perhaps, after the mauling, it proved difficult to inspire his men to the continued struggle against the Meccans, especially when they were called upon to fight in the sacred month when fighting was, by their old rules, forbidden.

> Fighting is obligatory to you (he had recorded in the Qu'ran), much as you dislike it. But you may hate a thing although it is good for you, and love a thing though it is bad for you. Allah knows, but you do not.

> They ask you about the sacred month. Say: To fight in this month is a grave offence; but to debar others from the path of Allah, to deny Him, and to expel

His worshippers from the Holy Mosque, is far more grave in His sight. Idolatry is worse than carnage.

They will not cease to fight against you until they force you to renounce your faith – if they are able. But whoever of you recants and dies an unbeliever, his works shall come to nothing in this world and in the world to come. Such men shall be the tenants of Hell, and there they shall abide for ever.

Those that have embraced the faith and those that have fled their land and fought for the cause of Allah, may hope for Allah's mercy. Allah is forgiving and merciful. [1]

Muhammad began to emerge as a leader in Medina, especially after he led the slaughter there of a large number of Jews. They were, it was said, sympathetic to the people of Mecca: it may have been that they had rejected Muhammad's message or, as monotheists, presented an alternative to the new faith. Muhammad took the battle to Mecca. He laid siege to it for a fortnight in 627. Three years later he entered the city at the head of an army of 10,000, meeting hardly any resistance. He had become the most successful of Arabia's chieftains. Tribes across the peninsula wished to acknowledge his leadership. If they did not, they laid themselves open to attack. The price of joining the federation of tribes was acceptance of Muhammad's role as the Prophet, the performance of prayers, and the payment of alms. They had, in other words, to adopt what later came to be known as Islam.

The attraction was not solely religious. Muhammad had harried the Meccans by attacking their convoys and carrying off their merchandise as booty. His soldiers were usually the victors, and grew rich on the proceeds of these raids. Others wanted to be part of this success. But there was a problem. Muhammad had proclaimed these, really quite traditional, activities of the tribesmen, as a "jihad", a holy war against those who had rejected the new faith: those who fought and died were promised a great reward, Paradise. [2] But a jihad could be fought only against non-Muslims. What therefore would happen when all the Arab tribes had adopted Islam? And how was he to keep the tribes, once they had adopted Islam, from the feuding which was endemic in their society: raids on convoys of traders was an example of this feuding. It was the perennial problem: what do you do with a demobilized army? Muhammad's answer was to keep them in the field. The jihad would continue to channel these martial energies and ensure the Muslim troops a proper supply of booty. But if it might be aimed only at non-Muslims it would have to be directed outside the Arabian peninsular.

It has already been said that Muhammad himself led only one, fairly brief, sortie outside the confines of Arabia. His successor, Abu Bakr, launched more. But it was under Abu Bakr's successor, Umar, that the Empire of Islam came into being. The fall of Damascus in 635 and of Jerusalem in 638 have been mentioned above. Ctesiphon, the summer capital of the Persian monarchs, fell in 636, and in 642 the Persians were completely overwhelmed at the Battle of Nihavand. The Byzantines suffered a similar fate at Heliopolis in Egypt, and Cyrus, the Patriarch of Alexandria, sued for peace – though only in 641 after the death of the Emperor Heraclius.

The progress of the armies of Islam was astonishing, and once more it seemed to those fighting in its cause irrefutable evidence that God was on their side in their holy war. The Byzantine Empire did not fall into the hands of the Muslims as had the Persian – the city of Constantinople withstood a siege by both land and sea from 674 to 677, and when the Muslims retreated they left, it was said, 30,000 of their number dead – but the occupation of Egypt left the way open to drive the Greeks from the coast of North Africa. The ancient city of Carthage was captured in 698 and by 705 the whole of the Mediterranean coast of Africa had been seized.

SPAIN

That left the way open to Spain. In 711 a freedman, Tariq, who had once belonged as a slave to Musa bin Nusayr, the governor of North Africa, crossed the straits of Gibraltar with a force of some 7,000 Berbers. Cordoba fell and so did Lisbon. In 712 he captured Toledo, capital of Visigothic Spain, and the Christian kingdom was destroyed. Tariq was joined in Toledo by his former owner, who claimed the Christian kingdom for Islam in the name of the Caliph in far-away Damascus. The governor then pressed on, advancing the frontiers of Islam as far as the Cantabrian Mountains, which guard the northern coast of the Iberian peninsular. Muslim forces were finally halted at Covadonga, by a nobleman called Pelayo. The date was probably 718. Pelayo's victory at Covadonga marked the beginning of the Christian Kingdom of Asturias, but to the east Muslim forces pressed onward over the Pyrenees into what is now France. Narbonne was taken and although the army was defeated at Toulouse in 721 by the Duke of Aquitaine, the Muslims still pushed forward until, in 732, they were defeated by Charles Martel in a battle near Poitiers. The Muslim forces were by that time over-stretched and the retreat began, but slowly: Narbonne was not abandoned – to Charles Martel's son Pepin – until 759. The reconquest of Spain by Christians was to take much longer.

Tariq himself – his name is commemorated in Gibraltar, Jabal Tariq – and his former master did not long remain in the country they had conquered. The Caliph

Charles Martel at the Battle of Poitiers

summoned them back to Damascus. They took a long time arriving, encumbered as they were with their Berber army, with Visigothic prisoners, and with rich booty. They were given a magnificent welcome, but their fame did not last. Both were to die in obscurity. Perhaps the Caliph, who in 717–781, while Tariq and Musa were capturing Spain for Islam, had launched yet another unsuccessful siege of Constantinople, was jealous.

Spain was to become one of the great triumphs of Islamic civilization — but it was also the first to break away from the Caliphate. In 644, as the second Caliph Umar lay dying after being stabbed by a Persian slave, he appointed a committee to select his successor. Of the two obvious candidates they chose Muhammad's father-in-law, Uthman, over his cousin and son-in-law Ali. Uthman himself was murdered in 656 and Ali succeeded after all, but he, too, was murdered. In 661 his opponent, Mu'awiya, governor of Syria, was proclaimed to be the Caliph, an event which took place in Jerusalem. He reorganized his court in the model of a quasi-imperial household, moving the capital of the Islamic Empire from Medina, which was now on the periphery of the Empire, to Damascus, which was at its heart. Jerusalem, where the Dome of the Rock was built to look like a (Christian) imperial basilica, was to become a new religious center, rivaling Medina and Mecca.

GOLDEN AGE

This was the beginning of the dynasty of the Umayyads. That dynasty survived until the very end of 749, when it was overthrown by the Abbasids, a family claiming descent from Muhammad's paternal uncle. They in their turn moved the capital from Damascus to Baghdad, and survived, though towards the end with very little power, until 1258 when Baghdad fell to the Mongol hordes under the grandson of Ghengis Khan, and the Caliph and many thousands of Baghdad's citizens were put to death.

But soon after the Umayyads were overthrown, one of its princes, Abd al-Rahman, fled to North Africa, and in 756 established himself in Cordoba, assuming the more modest title of "Emir" rather than that of Caliph. In 929, however, the Emir Abd al-Rahman III declared himself to be Caliph and ruled in great splendor. His reign gave

The cathedral in Murcia, Spain, was built on the site of a mosque

rise to a renaissance in Islamic theology, philosophy, astronomy, medicine and, as tourists can still see in the great mosque at Cordoba, in the architecture of Islam. It was a time of great tolerance towards, though not necessarily respect for, those of other faiths. But despite the tolerance extended to them many Christians and Jews in the Muslim part of Spain converted to Islam. Even those who did not convert chose to adopt Arabic language and culture: they were the Mozarabs, whose own form of Christian worship is still today performed in the cathedral at Toledo. But as with all golden ages, this one, too, was not to last. Tolerance came to an end under Abu Amir al-Mansur, or Almanzor, as he is known in the Spanish history books, who died in 1002. The Umayyads of Spain were overthrown in 1031, and in their place arose a scattering of kingdoms, petty principalities that were unable to resist the onslaught as Christians struggled to regain control of the Iberian peninsular. Toledo, the Visigoth capital, which fell to Tariq in 712, was taken by Alfonso VI, king of Leon and Castile, in 1085.

A mosque in Cordoba

The story of the final fall of Muslim Spain is told in a later part of this book. It was an untypical story. It was unusual because Islam was driven out of the Iberian peninsular, not because Muslim territory was fought over. On the contrary, compared with elsewhere in the Islamic world, Spain until the overthrow of the Umayyads had been relatively peaceful, at least in the south, allowing scholarship and literature to flourish as perhaps nowhere else in what is now mainland Europe. Scholarship flourished, too, in the Islamic heartlands. The urban civilization of the Near East, which had been in decline, revived after the Muslim conquests.

Baghdad, constructed by the Caliph al-Mansur (754–775) as the new capital city of the Abbasids, is thought to have grown to around one million inhabitants by the early ninth century, an extraordinary number, far in excess of urban populations elsewhere in the Near East or in Europe. It was rich from trade: Arabic as a lingua franca, together with the ties which bound Muslims together, made it far easier for merchants to travel from one end of the Empire to the other. As a literary culture Arabic was eventually joined, and perhaps even outshone, by Persian – but Persian was written in the Arabic script. In 830 the Caliph founded in Baghdad a kind of university, and Greek and Syriac texts were translated for the use of learned men – many of the classical texts that survive to this day owe their continued existence to the work done by Arab scholars. But they themselves were rarely the translators: they did not know Greek. Those who preserved and translated the documents were usually Eastern Christians living under Muslim rule. Similarly, Christians frequently held significant posts in the administration of the Islamic Empire, as John of Damascus and his father had done. It was a paradox, but without Christians and their skills the Islamic Empire could not have functioned so successfully.

This splendid culture far outdid anything in contemporary Europe. Latin texts were not translated (though the Qu'ran was translated into Latin) because Muslims considered Westerners as uncouth barbarians, and Western learning as of little worth. The degree of civilization was indeed high, but the empire of Islam which had produced it was inherently unstable. Some of the threats to its existence arose from the very way in which the Muslim world had been created. As early as the Caliphate of Uthman there was dissension, which, immediately after his death, broke out into civil war.

The problem was money. When in Medina the Prophet had won adherents to his new faith it was not so much by Islam's power to move the spirit as by Muhammad's success in harrying the rich caravans traveling to and from Mecca. His own, and his successors', campaigns outside Arabia were extensions of these skirmishes into a wider area. They had to provide the tribesmen who rallied to the cause of Islam with opportunities to enrich themselves at the expense of non-believers. And for a time they were remarkably successful. But then the Caliphs became victims of their own success. There were simply no more lands to conquer in the Near East. As a result there were fewer new sources of wealth with which to reward their troops – and as has been seen, though in

Above: A Mamaluke soldier

Below: Mamalukes exercising in the square of Mourad Bey Palace, Egypt, 1801

practice civil wars within Islam were not uncommon, they were forbidden to wage war on their co-religionists.

But there was also unrest about the way in which the recently acquired riches had been distributed. There were complaints that it was going to the already wealthy families of Mecca and Medina, rather than to the ordinary soldiers. There were further criticisms that not only were the spoils of war being distributed to the wealthy, too much of them were going to the family of the Caliph Uthman himself.

Those who profited from the Islamic conquests were predominantly Arabs. Over the centuries many in the Near East converted to Islam – by c. 850 Muslims were in the majority – but even if they had learnt to speak Arabic they did not enjoy the same rights and privileges as did those of Arab descent. There was frequently tension between

The ruins of Samarra

the Arabs and those of other ethnic groups. The Abbasid Caliph al-Mutasim (833–842) created a new army, made up of professionally trained soldiers. They were not Arabs but Turks, mainly slaves, or recently freed slaves: they were called Mamluks. As another symbol of his break with the past he moved his capital north of Baghdad, creating the new city of Samarra. The same pattern was repeated in Egypt itself, where, despite the immigration of Arabs, the Hellenistic culture of Christianity remained predominant for several centuries. But again the Arabs created a new capital, Fustat (Old Cairo), which developed out of a garrison town.

Ethnic tensions were particularly strong in Egypt, especially after its conquests by the Fatimids – so called, because Ubayd Allah, the founder of the dynasty, claimed descent from Ali's wife (and daughter of Muhammad) Fatima. Ubayd Allah had established control over most of North Africa, and had a great success especially among the Berbers in propagating his particular Ismaili version of Islam. With a Berber army Egypt was conquered in 969, and the Fatimids set up a new capital at al-Qahira (Cairo): the name means "the Victorious".

Under the Fatimids Egypt emerged as the most powerful state in the increasingly amorphous Islamic Empire. Its al-Azhar mosque became a major center of Islamic learning and culture. Overseen by (mostly) Christian viziers or chief ministers, Egypt's economy for a long time boomed, fed by tax revenue from the country's fertile farms, by gold from Nubia, and by trade passing through from the Yemen. It controlled an empire that included the Yemen, the Red Sea coast and much of Arabia, including Mecca. Palestine and Syria belonged to it. It governed North Africa and its fleet captured Sicily: Palermo surrendered in 831, though not until 966 did the island's former Byzantine masters concede their loss. In 874 Muslim troops reached Rome itself: the Leonine Walls, built the following year and taking their name from the Pope of the day, Leo IV, still survive as a reminder of the sacking of the papal city.

From the al-Azhar mosque the Fatimids exported their own, Ismaili form of Islam, though the Muslim population of Egypt, there before the coming of the Fatimids, stuck tenaciously to the Sunni creed. But it was weakened not so much, if at all, by diversity of belief as by ethnic conflicts between the Berbers, the Mamluks, and the black slaves, who formed distinct regiments in its army.

DIVISIONS

Division among Muslims, such as that between Sunnis and Ismailis, was another fault line in the seemingly invincible Islamic Empire. It was — and remains — a form of sectarianism similar to that experienced by Christian Churches. The Muslim sects differed in the degree of rigor with which they interpreted the Qu'ran. They differed in their attitude to proselytism, and therefore also in their attitude to Christians and other non-Muslims living within the borders of the Islamic state. But very often, if not invariably, the differences which separated one group from another reflected both ethnic realities and political interests.

The most significant, and long-lasting, division in Islam arose in the course of the struggle for the Caliphate between Ali, Muhammad's son-in-law, and Uthman, who was eventually chosen. When Uthman was assassinated in 656, Ali, who seized the Caliphate, was accused of being involved in Uthman's murder. He denied it, but agreed to arbitration. The decision of the arbiters went against him. He refused to accept it (the arbiters may indeed not have been entirely neutral) and massacred Muslims who criticized him for doing so.

Those who backed Ali's opponent Mu'awiya, became known as the Sunnis — the word means "consensus". Ali himself was murdered in 661, not by supporters of Mu'awiya but by the Kharijites, or "seceders". They believed that the whole notion of arbitration was wrong: only God could be the arbiter, and the Almighty's decision was made known through the judgment of the whole community. Only holiness of life mattered, they thought, and anyone who was in grave sin was outside the community of believers, was, in other words, an infidel and could be slain: Ali was their most prominent victim. Their apparently democratic principles made them attractive to those who had fallen foul of the government, and their active commitment to missionary work took Kharijites to the far corners of the Islamic world — including to the Berbers in Africa who were sympathetic to their rigorous doctrines. But they were only able to survive in the farthest reaches of the Muslim Empire.

The followers of Ali himself came to be called Shi'ites ("Shi'a" means "party"), though the Shi'ite "creed" itself only developed long after Ali's death. They grew in strength in the ninth and tenth centuries, drawing their support not so much from those of Arab descent, and therefore with a special relationship to the Prophet, but from converts to Islam, who resented the second-class status which was imposed upon them — and the higher taxes they had to pay for their humbler position. Their fundamental belief was that only a descendant of Ali could head the Islamic community — not as Caliph (Ali's son had resigned his claim to that title) but as an imam, a specifically religious leader. Some believed that the imam possessed secret knowledge, which each passed on to his successor. The "Twelver" faction thought that the line of imams had ended with the twelfth imam who, in 874 had, they believed, gone into hiding and would re-emerge as leader, or Mahdi, at some millenarian moment to bring justice to the world. The Ismailis, unlike the Twelvers, thought that the line of imams had survived among Ali's descendants, but who at any particular moment was imam might not always be known. The Ismailis were very active missionaries, especially among the North African Berbers. They were ripe for conversion: Berbers, after all, were not "People of the Book".

The "Book" is, of course, the Bible. In Muslim tradition, Muhammad was illiterate, and could not therefore have read the Old and New Testaments and borrowed from them. Nevertheless, there are similarities between the Qu'ran and the Jewish and Christian Scriptures. In the Qu'ran, for instance, there are nearly 100 references to Jesus who is presented as a righteous prophet, though to call him God, as in the Christian faith, is, according to Muhammad, to blaspheme. Christians and Jews were monotheists – though the doctrine of the Trinity was later to become one of the major issues of learned controversy between Muslim and Christians – so they were to that extent righteous. While one purpose of the jihad may have been to keep up the supply of new sources of wealth, another was to spread this new religious ideology called Islam, a message of monotheism and righteousness. "Right order" was to be imposed by the sword, as indeed it had been in Arabia in Muhammad's lifetime. Jews and, particularly, Christians were largely untouched except perhaps in the early conquest of Egypt: there were no forced conversions. Indeed, in the early years of the conquest Christian writers rarely if ever mention that the invaders had come propagating a distinctive religious faith. They may not have noticed. Pagans may have been coerced into accepting Islam, Jews and Christians were not. At least, not at first.

PUNISHMENT FOR SIN

When the Bishop of Jerusalem preached his Christmas Eve sermon in 634, with the Saracens (as he called them) camped around Bethlehem so Christians could not make their usual journey to the birthplace of Christ, he saw the coming of the Muslims as a punishment for the sins of his flock. He called the Muslims "godless", but he did not suggest that they belonged to another religion entirely. Nor would it have been strikingly obvious when, less than two years later, the Muslim army entered Jerusalem. The Caliph Umar, the story goes, entered a covenant (or "dhimma" – the people under the covenant were the "dhimmis") with the Christians. The text of the covenant, which follows, comes from a tenth-century source, and its authenticity is open to question –

Opposite: Church of the Holy Sepulchre, Jerusalem

as is the presence of Umar himself in Jerusalem (or Aelia, for the text uses the old Roman name for the city) in the aftermath of the conquest. Still, the regulations it lays down fairly represent the status of Christians.

> This is the guarantee granted the inhabitants of Aelia by the servant of God Umar, commander of the Believers.
>
> He grants them the surety of their persons, their goods, their churches, their crosses — whether these are in a good or bad condition — and the cult in general.
>
> Their churches shall not be expropriated for residences nor destroyed and their annexes will suffer no harm and the same will be true of their crosses and their goods.
>
> No constraint will be imposed upon them in the matter of their religion and no one of them will be annoyed.
>
> No Jew will be authorized to live in Jerusalem with them.
>
> It will be left to them to expel from the city the Byzantines and the brigands. Those of the latter who leave will have safe-conduct. Those who wish to stay will be authorized to do so, on condition of paying the same poll tax as the residents of Aelia.
>
> Those among the inhabitants of Aelia who wish to leave with the Byzantines, take with them their goods, leave behind their churches and their crosses, will likewise have a safe-conduct for themselves, their churches and their crosses . . .
>
> This writing is placed under the guarantee of God and the covenant of the Prophet, of the Caliphs and the Believers, on condition that the inhabitants of Aelia pay the poll tax that is incumbent upon them . . .[3]

Whether this text is authentic or not, it represents well a deal which would have been acceptable to the Christians. Umar is trying to win them over to support the expulsion of the Byzantines from Jerusalem, but that provision of the covenant Jerusalem's citizens probably did not regret. The Byzantines may have been their co-religionists, but they levied taxes that were higher than those the newly arrived Muslim authorities were imposing. They would not, therefore, have been particularly alarmed to see the Byzantines go. And the expulsion of the Jews was something the Christians had long wanted, but had failed to achieve. Jews, however, continued to reside in Jerusalem, whatever the terms of the covenant.

The situation, then, of "dhimmis", of those who had ceded their city to the Muslims under treaty, was unthreatening, certainly at first. They paid heavier taxes than those who eventually converted to Islam, but were not forced to change their faith. Their Arab conquerors, after all, needed their money. They were allowed to practice their religion in private, and to govern themselves according to their own communal laws – though it was always open to any party to a suit to appeal to a Muslim judge. And though in the very early days of the Muslim invasion it is clear that Christians had taken their side, they were exempt from military service.

But even from the first there were restrictions. Christians were not allowed to build or even to repair churches, though this ban was frequently overlooked by the Muslim authorities. They could not engage in public displays of their faith – go in processions, for example, carrying crosses. They were not allowed to wear white, a significant color for some Christians. They were not permitted to own Muslim slaves, though Muslims could own Christian ones, nor to give evidence in court against a Muslim. They had eventually to wear some distinctive form of dress to mark themselves off as Christians, a prescription that became more severe as time went by. And, naturally, they were forbidden to proselytize.

Such rules were not all imposed everywhere, and at all times, with the same degree of severity. They were more likely to be enforced in the cities than in the countryside, and in Syria the second Muslim century was more hostile to Christians than the first had been: under the Caliph Mutawakkil (847–861) the hostility amounted to outright persecution. Christians were forbidden to hold government offices – though a Christian was majordomo of Mutawakkil's own palace. They were even banned from learning Arabic. The Caliph was, it should be said, just as severe

The citadel at Aleppo dates from the 12th and 13th centuries, at the height of Arab military architecture

upon those of his own faith, enforcing his own notion of a strict Muslim orthodoxy.

In Spain the worst persecution came a century after that, under Almanzor. With his army of Berbers he campaigned against Christians in the north of the Iberian peninsular. He pillaged churches, and insisted that they be kept open night and day to accommodate any Muslim traveler who might be passing. Christian cemeteries were not permitted near Muslim ones, and funeral processions were forbidden anywhere near Muslim areas. Not only could Christians not speak of their faith to Muslims, they were forbidden even to read the Qu'ran. Any Muslim who converted to Christianity was condemned to death — a law within Islam still in operation today. In public places

Christians were obliged to give way to Muslims. Areas were designated for Christian dwellings. Even their homes were required to be lower than those of Islamic households. A century later these laws were imposed in North Africa. A century after that and Muslim Spain was almost defeated. Laws very similar to those that had regulated the behavior of Christians in a Muslim state now began to be applied to Muslims in a Christian one.

Between European rulers and the Caliphs there were occasional formal contacts. In 797, for instance, the King of the Franks, Charlemagne, not yet Emperor, sent an embassy to the court of Harun al-Rashid. As a result privileges were granted to clergy serving the churches in Jerusalem, and a hostel was established there for those pilgrims who had continued to travel to the Holy Land, despite it being under the control of Muslims.

The Emperor Charlemagne

In the centuries before the crusades, however, few Muslims knew, or cared, much about Christianity even though Christians frequently occupied the highest administrative posts in their governments. And while Christians in the East and in Spain might know a fair amount about Islam, little was known in the Western world generally. The fall of Toledo to a Christian king in 1085 began to change that. Islamic writings became available to Western scholars, who traveled to Toledo to learn Arabic. They were able to gain a more balanced view of this alien faith.

But the wider population of Europe had a wholly different perspective from that of the scholars, fed as it was by romantic epics such as the *Song of Roland*, best known of all the *chansons de geste*. The *chansons*, sung by court minstrels, told of the daring deeds of knights, and especially of knights associated with Charlemagne. Usually these were fictional deeds, though the *Song of Roland* has an element of truth. In 778 Charlemagne led an army into Spain. He reached as far as Zaragossa, but the Muslims refused to surrender the city to the Franks, and Charlemagne had to fall back across the Pyrenees when he learnt that his German territories were under attack from the Saxons. In the pass of Roncesvalles his army was attacked, and many leading noblemen died in the battle.

In the chansons which grew out of this disaster, Charlemagne had entered Spain to help Christians who were suffering under the Muslims; when Charlemagne retreats, Roland heroically defends his ground against the Muslim army, which treacherously ambushes the king's soldiers. The enemy was not only vicious and violent, they were also deceitful: Charlemagne's forces had been led into a trap, and the rearguard, commanded by Roland, was overcome by vastly superior forces. It is a story of noble and virtuous Christians (though there are some traitors among them) and perfidious Muslims.

But it did not happen. At least, it did not happen like that. When Charlemagne led his army into Spain he did so at the request of some Muslim emirs; his whole army

– and not just the rearguard – was thrown into disarray at Roncesvalles. It is also true that many of them died, including many noblemen – the "paladins" of the legends. The attackers, however, were not Muslims but for the most part Christian Basques – though there may have been some Muslims as well.

The story of Roland had been circulating in ballads of one form or another from the ninth century. But it did not take its classic form, the form in which it has come down to us, until the eleventh century. Within the Islamic Empire the eleventh century was a time both of religious and political turmoil.

Roland at Roncesvalles

First there was the resurgence of Persia, and a period of relative stability led to missionary efforts among the Turks, the new migrants into the Near East with their flocks and their possessions. But in 1004 the Turks turned on the Persian dynasty and overthrew it. Their leader moved his capital to Afghanistan, and every year pushed further and further into India, forcibly converting as he went. At the other end of the eleventh century, the triumph of Christianity over Muslims in Spain was short-lived. Yusuf ibn Tashfin invaded from North Africa, in 1086 decisively defeating Alfonso VI. And although the cultured Muslims of Spain despised both his uncouth Berber army and his own fundamentalist interpretation of his faith, ibn Tashfin once more established Islamic rule over much of the peninsular.

The biggest crisis, however, came at the beginning of the eleventh century, and it was a crisis not just for the West but for Islam as well. It was the accession to the Fatimid (Egyptian) Caliphate in 996 of al-Hakim. It should have been the occasion for mild optimism by Christians: al-Hakim had a Christian mother. Indeed, his reign started well. A resurgent Byzantium was threatening to recapture Palestine and restore the Holy Places to Christian control, but al-Hakim was able to agree a truce on the grounds that he was a moderate. His moderation, however, swiftly disappeared. In 1003, two years after the truce, he began persecuting Christians in Egypt. He destroyed churches. He built over sacred places, shrines and burial grounds. The surviving churches were ordered to have mosques built on their roofs. Then, six years later, he turned his attention to Jerusalem. The account that follows is from an eleventh-century historian of Antioch. He was a Christian, and therefore not an unbiased observer, but the basic facts are not in dispute:

> al-Hakim likewise sent to Syria, to Yarukh, governor of Ramle, written orders to destroy the Church of the Holy Resurrection, to get rid of Christian emblems and to destroy completely the Christian relics. Yarukh sent to Jerusalem his son Yusuf and Husayn ibn Zahir, the inspector of currency, with Abu al-Fawaris al-Dayf. They confiscated all the furnishings that were in the church, after which they razed it completely, except those parts that were impossible to destroy or would have been too difficult to carry away. The

Cranion [Golgotha, the place of Christ's death] was destroyed, as well as the Church of St Constantine and everything that was found in the precinct. The complete destruction of the relics was accomplished. Ibn Zahir bent every effort to demolish the Holy Sepulchre and to remove its every trace; he broke up the greater part of it and removed it. In the neighborhood of the Holy Sepulchre there was a convent of women called Dayr al-Sari, which he likewise destroyed. The demolition began on [28 September 1009]. All the goods and endowed possession belonging to the church were seized, as well as all the cult object and gold ornaments. [4]

It is not clear what aroused al-Hakim's ire against the Christian holy places. A Muslim historian a little afterwards put it down to the event each Easter in the Church of the Holy Sepulchre, when new fire, it was said, was miraculously kindled by God himself. It was on hearing about this bit of trickery, said the historian, that he was incited to act. In the end thousands of churches were destroyed in Egypt, Palestine and Syria.

In 1016 the Caliph had another change of heart. He restored their possessions to the Christians, declared himself divine, and started persecuting Muslims instead. In 1021 al-Hakim simply disappeared from history, in all probability murdered at the instigation of his sister. The Church of the Holy Sepulchre was rebuilt. The Christians in Jerusalem carried on much as before, and the number of pilgrims to the Holy Places increased.

But how well were they treated? A vast German pilgrimage, many thousands, it seems, led by the Bishop of Bamberg, arrived in the Holy Land in 1064. There were rich pickings to be had by brigands – and they were taken: there was not only a robbery but a massacre. Then, in 1071 Palestine fell to new rulers, the Seljuk (the name comes from one of their early leaders) Turks. The Christian historian William of Tyre, born and bred in Palestine, wrote:

When the power of the Turks began to flourish, and their sway was extended over the lands of the Egyptians and Persians, matters grew worse again. The Holy City came under their control and, during the 28 years of Turkish

Opposite: The burial place of Jesus inside the Church of the Holy Sepulchre, Jerusalem

domination, the people of God endured far greater troubles, so that they came to look back upon as light the woes which they had suffered under the yoke of the Egyptians and Persians.[5]

Perhaps the regime of the Seljuks was indeed worse than that of the Fatimids, al-Hakim apart. But William was writing almost a century after the situation he describes, and other sources do not suggest that Christians were particularly being persecuted. Perhaps that was the kind of propaganda that may have been circulating in Europe and which helped to inspire the crusade. But there was another dramatic turn, which had far more influence on subsequent events.

In March 1071 at Manzikert, near Lake Van in Armenia, the Turkish Seljuk Sultan, Alp Arslan, went into battle with the Byzantine army under the Emperor Romanus. The Byzantine army, composed largely of mercenaries, was utterly defeated and the Emperor captured. For the conquering Muslims the way lay open into Anatolia, into territories that had always hitherto been Christian. The way lay open for a Muslim army to march to the threshold of the ancient Christian capital, Constantinople. The Emperor Alexius Commenus desperately needed help, military assistance, from the West.

The scene was set for the outbreak of a Western, Christian holy war against the forces of Islam.

---

1. *The Koran*, translated by N. J. Dawood (London: Penguin Books, 1983), pp. 354–55 (Suras 2:216-217).

2. It is perhaps worth commenting that the word "jihad" means "striving", and though it is often interpreted as being the equivalent of fighting, later, more mystical, forms of Islam suggested that the chief striving was against oneself.

3. Quoted in *Jerusalem*, by F. E. Peters (Princeton NJ: Princeton University Press, 1985), pp. 185–186.

4. Ibid., p. 260.

5. Ibid., p. 250.

Chapter Three

Crusades

*I*n the late summer of 1095 Pope Urban II went home to France. He had been born about the year 1035 in Châtillon-sur-Marne, just west of Epernay. Odo de Lagery was noble by birth. He studied in Rheims, and became a canon of the cathedral there and eventually archdeacon, but in c. 1068 he joined the great abbey of Cluny. He rose to be Grand Prior, and then entered papal service. About the year 1080 Pope Gregory VII made him Cardinal Bishop of Ostia, and sent him as his representative, or legate, to Germany. This was a dangerous task. The German King – soon to be crowned Emperor by an anti-pope – was effectively at war with Gregory, and after Gregory's death so confused were the late pope's supporters that it was almost a year before they could elect a successor – who survived less than a year.

Odo was elected Pope in March 1088 at Terracina, a town south of Rome, because the city itself was in the hands of an anti-pope. It was 1093 before he was able finally to enter the city, and another year before he gained control of his cathedral church of St John Lateran. Even then he had to use bribery. The problem was reform of the Church, to which Gregory VII had been deeply committed, and in which Pope Urban II was Gregory's devoted disciple. His two years of travel through Italy and France before going back to Rome were to foster the program that Gregory had set in place, and to insist, in particular, on the independence of the Church from kings and other magnates.

In November 1095 he held a council in Clermont, in central France. Reforming decrees were once more issued, but even more starkly than before. Bishops and priests were forbidden to become vassals of any lay person, whether king or merely noble. This was what Gregory VII would have wished – but it was far more demanding that he had himself ever dared implement.

And then, on 27 November, he preached a sermon.

> Oh race of Franks, we learn that in some of your provinces no one can venture on the road by day or by night without injury or attack by highwaymen, and no one is secure even at home. Let us then re-enact the law of our ancestors known as the Truce of God. And now that you have promised to maintain the peace among yourselves you are obliged to succor your brethren in the East, menaced by an accursed race, alienated from God. The Holy Sepulchre of Our Lord is polluted by the filthiness of an unclean nation. Recall the greatness of Charlemagne. Oh most valiant soldiers, descendants of invincible ancestors, be not degenerate. Let all hatred depart from among you, all quarrels end, all wars cease. Start upon the road to the Holy Sepulchre to wrest that land from the wicked race and subject it to yourselves.

No text of the sermon survives;[1] the above is one version of what was preached, an amalgam of hints in various sources. There are five known accounts of what Urban said, which were written within a quarter of a century or so of the Council of Clermont. One of those recording his words was certainly present, others may have been. But all were writing in the light of what happened next. Though they may have the gist of what the Pope said, the exact words are impossible now to recover. What is unquestioned, however, is that Pope Urban's sermon launched what has come to be known as the first crusade.

And that is remarkable because, as has been seen in the opening chapter, until the very eve of the launch of the first crusade, the Church had seemed to be steadfastly opposed to violence. Now, however, attitudes had changed. An encyclical letter was forged at the Cluniac abbey of Moissac shortly after Urban had visited there on his way back to Rome from Clermont. Attributed to Sergius IV, pope between 1009 and

1012, it called upon Christian warriors to exterminate the enemies of God who were guilty of destroying the Holy Sepulchre. Nothing could have been a starker invitation to battle, so what had happened to change the Church's stance toward warfare?

A REFORMING POPE

What happened was Pope Gregory VII. The great reforming pope, Urban's mentor, was elected in April 1073. A year or so later he was engaged in gathering an army to go to the aid of the Byzantine Emperor Michael VII Ducas, whose Christian lands in Asia Minor were being devastated by the Seljuk Turks. Not only that, but he was proposing to lead it himself. This would not be the first time a pope had led his troops into battle against the forces of Islam, but hitherto it had happened only in Italy, and in self-defense.

Pope Gregory VII

Gregory's intention may have been to relieve pressure on Byzantium, but he was also concerned, and perhaps more so, to bring about a reunion between the two churches of Rome and Constantinople. In 1054 they had hurled anathemas at one another, but it is only with hindsight that we recognize that event as a definitive break between East and West. It certainly did not seem so to Gregory, and he thought that military assistance against the advance of the Seljuks would aid the process of reconciliation.

Never had the Byzantines so needed help. In 1071 at Manzikert in Eastern Anatolia, on a plain not far from Lake Van, they had suffered their most crushing defeat ever at the hands of Islam. It was made all the worse because it was unnecessary: the Seljuk Sultan was already withdrawing, but the Byzantine Emperor had cut him off from his homeland. Alp Arslan consequently had no alternative but to engage the troops of the Emperor Romanus Diogenes. In the ensuing battle not only were the Byzantines decisively defeated — it was ever after referred to as "that Dreadful Day" — but Romanus himself was captured, the very first time a Byzantine Emperor had fallen into enemy hands.

Gregory's plans to raise an army came to nothing. They were not very far advanced when he had to abandon them because of too many other concerns – his relationship with the German King Henry IV, and with the Normans in Southern Italy and Sicily. But the idea had been sown, and Gregory took his military aspirations further. In a letter to the Abbot of Cluny he broached the idea of mobilizing all the Knights of Europe in some kind of holy militia. Such soldiers might even, he suggested, use force against those of the clergy who resisted his Church reforms. It was only a step from that to the idea of holy war. As a ruler of the papal states, he was of course obliged to concern himself in their military defense. But so had been every other pope for half a millennium. When Popes Leo IV (d. 855) and John VIII (d. 882, perhaps assassinated by one of his entourage,) appealed to the Franks to defend Rome from Saracen attacks, they promised Paradise to those who might die in the battle to protect the patrimony of St Peter. The liturgy had already for a century or so contained prayers both for the blessing of swords and for the soldiers themselves, praying that, in fighting, they might

Pope Leo IV

have the right intention. Gregory's close collaborator, Anselm of Lucca, even argued, though it was still against the run of theological opinion and ecclesiastical practice, that those who killed committed no sin, always provided they had the right motive in doing so. Gregory went further. When preparing the ground for his army to go to the aid of the Byzantines, he appears to suggest that death in such a godly enterprise would be the equivalent of martyrdom, and earn the fallen a place in heaven.

But none of this was clear cut. In 1078 a synodal decree approved by Gregory insisted that knighthood, because it involved shedding blood, was a career that could not be followed without committing sin. That was teaching which was faithful to the Church's tradition. Yet even by insisting on it, Gregory prepared the way for the crusade, because he made the knightly class conscious of their sinfulness, and therefore of their need for penance. The time-honored way of doing penance was by becoming a monk but, as the chronicler of the first crusade, the abbot Guibert de Nogent, remarked, God had instituted "holy warfare" so that knights in order to save their souls would not have to abandon their accustomed way of life. By going on what was, in effect, an armed pilgrimage to Jerusalem, they could by use of their weapons perform the penance required of them. It was a powerful motive in attracting knights to answer Pope Urban's summons. "Let robbers become soldiers of Christ," said Pope Urban. And, he promised, if anyone loses his life, whether en route to the Holy Land or in Jerusalem, "his sins shall be remitted." [2]

This, as has been seen, was not a wholly new idea. Previous popes had made similar statements, including Gregory VII. Indeed, whereas earlier popes had spoken in such terms only in situations where they were defending their territory against Muslims, Gregory had gone further and had proposed taking the holy war into the enemy camp. There were a number of factors, however, which made Urban's appeal distinctive.

First of all, it seems to have been addressed specifically to the French, the Franks, Urban's fellow-countrymen, and in the context of the Peace of God which, should it be observed (and efforts were made to see that it was) would make it safe for the French nobility to leave their territories and go on this military, penitential, exercise. Secondly, this was "taking the cross", a direct reference to Christ's command to the devout to "take up his cross and follow me". The wearing of the cross upon a knight's dress came to mark him out as a crusader. Thirdly and most importantly, it was associated with a vow. This later became formalized in the Church's canon law, but it was formal enough a year after Urban's sermon for the clergy who had joined the Christian army to excommunicate those who had taken the vow in the aftermath of the Pope's appeal, and then failed to fulfill it.

The vow had been suggested by Pope Urban more than six months earlier, in March, at the Council of Piacenza. The Byzantine Emperor had sent envoys to the Pope at Piacenza to persuade the West to provide him with a company of knights to defend what remained of the Empire. Emperor Alexius had already had experience of Western mounted soldiery: a small company had been supplied to him by Count Robert of Flanders, and their military skills had been much admired. He wanted more of the same. What he did not want was what he got, a huge army intent not on recovering the lands lost in Anatolia after the disastrous battle of Manzikert, but on regaining for Christianity possession of the Holy Sepulchre in Jerusalem.

What he got first of all, however, was hardly an army at all. In the spring of 1096 peasants right across Europe hurriedly harvested their crops, packed their family, food and belongings into wagons, and set off. What attracted them may have been the promise by the Pope that by going on the crusade they could purge all the punishment still awaiting them in the next world for the sins which had been forgiven in this. It may also have been the hope that by leaving the lands they tilled to fight in this holy war they would achieve the status of freemen, perhaps, it has been suggested, even set themselves up as farmers in the new territories they believed they were about to liberate from the Muslims. Or perhaps it was just a deep religious fervor.

Whatever the reason, they went in their thousands – from 50,000 to 70,000, it has been estimated, set off between April and June. They were rallied by Peter the Hermit of Amiens, a wandering preacher of penance, and set out in some half dozen successive waves. They made their disorderly way through Germany, Bohemia, and Hungary – the conversion of which to Christianity in the late tenth century had made a land route to the Holy Land possible, and given impetus to the Jerusalem pilgrimage.

Though they were setting off to fight the forces of Islam, these peasant warriors first set about destroying non-Christians within their own lands. As they passed through Cologne, Worms, Speyer and Prague – among other places – they systematically put to death the Jewish communities of these towns. The would-be crusaders (though the term was not yet in use) ran amok, slaughtering any Jew they might find, frequently despite the efforts of churchmen to prevent them by giving sanctuary to the Jews. It was a pogrom of appalling ferocity.

As they marched on they ran out of food, and began to loot the countryside they passed through. In Hungary they were harried by troops trying to keep some sort of control, and likewise when they entered the Balkans and Byzantine territory. Alexius tried to curb their rampage by giving them food, but still they destroyed villages, and slew villagers, as they made their way to Constantinople. Peter the Hermit was still with them. In Constantinople he managed to establish some sort of control, but the Emperor was unwilling to put up with this rabble. He hurriedly transported them out of his city and across the Bosphorus. At Nicaea, modern Iznik, they encountered the enemy they had marched so far to fight. The few nobles who were with them, and Peter the Hermit himself, counseled caution. The peasant army would have none of it, went into battle, and was almost totally destroyed.

Back in Europe the nobles and their retainers, the audience which Pope Urban had been addressing, took longer to set off. They needed time to put their affairs in order or, for many of them, to raise the money to pay for their expedition. There were four groups as they made their way east. Those from Britain were Norman knights:

Peter the Hermit leading the Crusades

men, or descendants of men, who had conquered England just over 30 years previously. They naturally joined their Norman relatives from northwest France. Knights from northern France and Lorraine were joined by a contingent from Flanders. There was an army from southern France and one constituted by the Normans who had settled in southern Italy. Most took the overland route that the peasants' crusade had traversed six months earlier; some, especially those from southern Italy, went by sea to the Balkans, and then by land. One at a time, the armies reached Constantinople.

Alexius was naturally happier with the new arrivals than he had been with the peasant army, but it was still not what he had been expecting. So large a force could have been as much a threat to the integrity of what was left of the Byzantine Empire as it was to the Muslims. He again provided transport to get them across the Bosphorus, but not before extracting from their leaders an oath of loyalty.

Once in Asia Minor the new arrivals arrived, as Peter the Hermit had done, at the city of Nicaea occupied by the Seljuk Turks. It had walls six kilometers long but, more significant as far as siege went, it was partly on Lake Ascania and could be re-victualled by water. And so it was, until the Byzantines provided the Christian army with boats. The Seljuks withdrew, unwilling to face the crusaders in open battle. Once Nicaea had fallen the Christian army marched on to do battle again at Dorylaeum (Eskisehir) on 1 July 1097, and then onwards again to Iconium (Konya).

This was in the heat of the summer. Supplies provided by the Byzantines were running out, and there was little to be had by foraging in the countryside through which they passed. More particularly they were short of water, and many, if not most, of the horses died on the journey. They found water at Iconium, however, and the countryside was soon to become more fertile. They reached Herclea (Eregli). There they divided, one group going by a northerly route, another taking a more hazardous but more direct southerly one. They met up again at Marash (Maras).

At Marash there was a further division. Baldwin, brother of Godfrey of Bouillon, marched east to Edessa (Urfa), in response to appeals from the large

Opposite: Crusaders attack Nicaea

A view of Antioch

Christian population of the region. He captured Edessa and took it over: the County of Edessa became the first crusader principality.

In October, four months after leaving Constantinople and two years after Pope Urban's summons, the crusaders were on the borders of the Holy Land, laying siege to the city of Antioch. Antioch (Antkya), fortified by the Byzantine Emperor Justinian four and a half centuries before, was a formidable challenge. The siege lasted until the beginning of June 1098. By June the Christian army was threatened by the Muslim leader Kerbogha, the Atabeg of Mosul, at the head of an army of Iraqi and Persian troops. The situation of the Christians was desperate. They were saved only by an act of treachery within Antioch: one of the defending captains allowed the crusaders to scale his section of the walls unmolested under cover of darkness. By the end of the following day all of Antioch except the citadel was in Christian hands, though they were now trapped within it as Kerbogha's army took up camp outside the walls. The besiegers had become the besieged.

A MIRACULOUS VISION

At first the crusaders pinned their hopes for relief on the Emperor Alexius. He was leading an army to support them, but when he believed himself threatened (some accounts suggest that he had heard the crusaders had been decisively defeated so it was useless to proceed) he turned back. The crusaders never forgave him, and it made a permanent rift between Byzantium and most – though not quite all – of the Western invaders of the Holy Land.

Morale was low. The expedition might have ended in ignominious failure at Antioch on the Orontes had it not been for an obscure Provençal cleric called Peter Bartholomew. A vision guided him to a hidden lance, which, he claimed, was the very lance with which the side of Christ had been pierced at the crucifixion. This was a great boost to the crusaders' morale. It was also the case that the army of Kerbogha, not accustomed to prolonged sieges, was in the process of breaking up. Almost a month after taking Antioch the crusaders marched out again to do battle, led by the Holy Lance and encouraged by a vision of St George. The Muslim army fled.

The Christian army stayed on in Antioch for a further six months. This delay was a mistake on many counts. There was an epidemic of typhoid during which many died, among them Bishop Adhemar of Le Puy, the only person who could exercise some degree of authority over the whole motley army. His loss was a grievous blow. The leaders squabbled among themselves as to who was in charge. More seriously, the Fatimids from Egypt, seeing the disarray of the Seljuk Turks, marched northwards and captured Jerusalem for themselves. It was not until mid January 1099, and only then at the prompting of the ordinary soldiers rather than at the wishes of the leaders, that the crusading army marched out of Antioch and once more took the road to Jerusalem. By the time it arrived there, on 7 June, it amounted to some 1,200 mounted soldiers (knights) and about 10,000 foot soldiers. At the siege of Nicaea not quite two years earlier, there had been three times the number, but some had died, in battle or from disease, some had settled in Antioch or elsewhere, and some had returned home.

Within Jerusalem the Egyptian governor prepared for a siege. Around the city he pursued a scorched earth policy, destroying food sources and poisoning wells. He also expelled all Christians from Jerusalem, making it easier to keep the remaining Muslim and Jewish inhabitants supplied, and increasing the difficulties for the besieging army who now had to feed extra mouths.

The crusaders' tactics were both spiritual and military. They fasted, did penance, and processed barefoot round the walls. They also prepared siege engines out of sight of the Muslim defenders. It was impossible for them wholly to enclose the city, their numbers being too few, so an assault on the city was inevitable. It occurred on 14 and 15 July. The Muslim defenders fell back to the Temple Mount, and there surrendered. The governor was escorted out of the city, while over the next three days the Muslims were slaughtered. William of Tyre, who admittedly was not an eyewitness, put the number of Muslim dead at 10,000 on the Temple Mount alone. Fulcher of Chartres was there at Christmas. The bodies of the dead Saracens, he said, still lay where they had fallen. The stench was horrendous. Jews died alongside the Muslims, though some were held for ransom, and others fled to safe havens. The crusaders simply took over the houses of those they had slain or had driven out. "In this way,"

Jerusalem and the Dome of the Rock

This ancient Greek mosaic map of the world has Jerusalem at its centre

remarked Fulcher, "many poor people became wealthy." [3]

The crusaders, meanwhile, entered the church of the Holy Sepulchre and sang a Te Deum.

Jerusalem was taken, but the struggle for the Holy Land was not yet over. Gradually the coastal towns fell to the crusaders. Most had been captured by IIII, but Tyre held out until II24. When it came, that was an important victory because it meant the Egyptian fleet was unable to sail northwards along the coast, and so made it safer for fleets from Europe to reach the Holy Land.

A juridical structure had also to be established. The first ruler chosen declined the role. The second, Godfrey of Lower Lotharingia, declared himself only to be Guardian of the Holy Sepulchre. But he died soon afterwards and in II00 his brother Baldwin, who had no such scruples, was crowned as the first king of the Latin Kingdom of Jerusalem, to which was added, in a loose federation, the County of Tripoli, the County of Edessa, and the Principality of Antioch.

News of the triumph had, naturally, reached Europe. Urban II died two weeks after the taking of Jerusalem. The new Pope, Paschal II, heard the news shortly after his election. He, like his predecessor, urged those who had taken the vow but had not gone to the Holy Land, or who had gone but had returned, or those who simply had

not yet decided to go, to take the cross — the ceremony of being invested with a cross to mark crusader status seems to date from Paschal's pontificate. Three huge armies set out — at least as many as had set off in 1097 departed again in 1100–1101. They reached Constantinople but were, once more, swiftly moved on by the Emperor Alexius. Though some individuals and small groups reached Jerusalem, the armies themselves were systematically destroyed by the Seljuks as they crossed Anatolia. It was a warning that the success of the first wave of crusaders was to be attributed at least as much to the disunity among their Muslim adversaries as it was to their own military prowess. The crusaders' hold over the Holy Land was to be precarious. There were, reported Fulcher of Chartres, only 300 knights and about the

Above: The castle walls at Acre

Below: The ancient harbour at Joppa, now known as Jaffa

same number of foot soldiers available for the defense of the Holy City.

Nonetheless, pilgrims continued to arrive at the Holy Places. And this was despite the insecurity, which in practice was probably no worse than during the eleventh century when there had been a considerable expansion of the numbers making their way to Jerusalem from all parts of Europe. The numbers had grown because of the opening of the land route, but the sea route continued to be used. The nearest disembarcation point to Jerusalem was Jaffa (Tel Aviv-Yafo). Its port, however, was not thought safe. Acre (Akko) was a better harbor, and was taken by the crusaders in 1104. There were, eventually, other ports of entry, but Jaffa was the main one, and all pilgrims, no matter were they landed, made their way there, and then onwards to the Holy City.

It was always a perilous journey. Not long – four years or so – after Jerusalem had fallen to the Christians, an Englishman called Saewulf made his way there, and wrote an account of his experiences. He went from Jaffa, or Joppa as it was also known. He commented on the danger from the Saracens, who lay in wait in the caves along the mountain path. They would attack small groups of pilgrims, or stragglers on the route. The pilgrims needed protection. It was to defend them that the Templars came into existence.

MASSACRE

Just when, or how, this happened is not recorded. Shortly before Easter 1119 a group of 300 pilgrims were killed, recounted a contemporary chronicler, and a further 60 taken into captivity by the Saracens. As the beginning of the Templars (though this name as such was not used until the 1140s) is certainly about this time, it is possible that the massacre of the Christians was the catalyst.

Leader of the group of knights who were the founding members of the Templars was Hugh de Payen. His village of Payen is just north of Troyes, in Champagne; his liege lord was Count Hugh of Champagne, who himself became a knight of the Temple in 1125. Hugh de Payen may have been in the Holy Land in 1104 when Count Hugh was there. Though he returned to France, he went back again to the Holy Land, possibly in 1116. How the decision was taken to form a group of

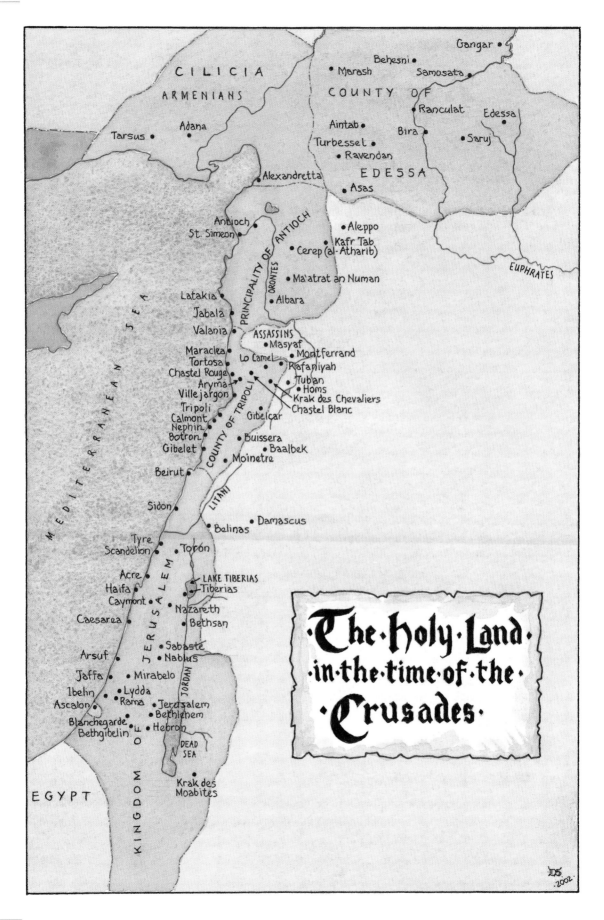

knights who would be both quasi monks, taking vows of poverty, chastity and obedience, and at the same time warriors has not been recorded. There were in Europe small associations, "confraternities" to use a religious term, of knights who banded together for a particular religious purpose, but these associations demanded only temporary membership and did not turn their members into monks. What Hugh de Payen was proposing was something entirely new, which, in the eyes of many churchmen, made it highly suspect. The new knighthood already had secular approval: King Baldwin I had given them accommodation in a section of his own palace on the

Temple Mount (hence the name of the Order). It was now essential to get ecclesiastical approval. There is a suggestion that he got local approval at a council held in Nablus in 1120. But for wider recognition it was necessary for Hugh de Payen, as "Master" of the Order, to travel back to Europe.

Hugh returned to Europe in 1126. He came seeking new recruits – William of Tyre, in a suspiciously neat turn of phrase, says that

Cultivating the land of Citeaux Abbey in France

there were only nine members for the first nine years. But Hugh also attended the Council of Troyes. The Council opened in January 1128. It was a local council, attended by two archbishops, sundry abbots, and a papal legate. One of the abbots, however, was the redoubtable St Bernard of Clairvaux.

Bernard was one of the most powerful figures of the medieval Church. He had been born near Dijon in 1190 into a noble family who might have expected him to follow the career of a knight. Instead, when he was 22, he persuaded some of his brothers and other men of equal rank – 31 in all – to join the abbey of Citeaux, at the time almost on the point of collapse. His action changed the fortunes of the monastery: by the time Bernard died in 1153 (he was declared a saint – canonized – only 21 years later), Citeaux had founded right across Europe some 500 houses of monks. The Cistercians – as the religious Order was called after the name of the mother house of Citeaux – followed a very strict rule of life, and their houses, and their churches, were distinguished by the simplicity of their architecture and the plainness of their ornamentation. The monks themselves wore a white habit.

Bernard, however, did not stay in Citeaux itself. In 1115, on land granted by Count of Hugh of Champagne, he founded the abbey of Clairvaux, and it was as

The Inner Temple, London

abbot of Clairvaux that he attended the Council at Troyes. And at Troyes Hugh de Payen was given a rule of life for the military Order he had founded. It had many similarities to the rule adopted by the Cistercians, even down to the white habit (though the knights were at the time allowed also black or brown).

The manner of life, or rule, of the Templars, and of the other Orders of Knighthood that came to be founded, will be discussed in a later chapter (see below, pp. 155-168). For the moment what is significant are two other documents, probably written between 1129 and 1135. One of them, entitled *De laude novae militiae* ("In praise of the new knighthood") was undoubtedly written by St Bernard of Clairvaux. The other, unlike Bernard's work which was clearly much copied, exists in only one manuscript. It is earlier than Bernard's short treatise, and is a letter by one Hugh "the sinner". Who this Hugh may be is uncertain. It could possibly have been Hugh de Payen himself, though nothing we know of him suggests that he was capable of composing a letter of spiritual guidance in Latin. One other possible author is a Hugh who was a theologian at the abbey of St Victor in Paris. The rule of life of this house of Augustinian canons had been much influenced by Bernard, which could be a connection between this Victorine and the Templars. But there is no other reason to suppose Hugh of St Victor had any interest in the new Order, and the Latin, which would probably have been too difficult for Hugh de Payen, is far too simple for the learned theologian.

It would be interesting to know who was the letter's author because of the argument that it puts forward. It reverses the Church's traditional hostility to warfare, at least in certain circumstances — namely, warfare against the Muslims, or Saracens. Hugh, whoever he was, says that a knight does not kill out of anger. The Devil tempts him to do so, and that would be sinful, but it is possible, he suggests, following St Augustine, to kill justly.

Though still relatively short, Bernard's exhortation is much more expansive than Hugh's. Playing on the contrast between *malitia* (evil) and *militia* (knighthood), it is aimed primarily — just like Hugh's — at fostering the spiritual life of the Templars, which, at the Council of Troyes, had been encapsulated in their new rule. However, the way Bernard starts suggests that there were those who were unhappy at this strange hybrid. It is not odd, he says, that people should fight a flesh-and-blood adversary: that is common enough. And it is not odd that some people should fight a spiritual foe: the world, he remarks, is full of monks. What is novel is the combination of both in the same group of men. There is nothing more glorious than to die when fighting against the enemies of Christianity, because to do so is to die a martyr. "The Christian glories in the death of the pagan," he says, "because Christ is glorified." Someone who kills an evil-doer, he adds, is no murderer: what he is doing is killing evil. Bernard seems to have himself felt he was going perhaps a little too far because he is at pains to insist that pagans should not be killed unless there is no other way of preventing them persecuting Christians. But, he says, it is better to kill them than let them rule over Christians.

This is, of course, a defense of killing "pagans", and not a defense of war in general. Bernard is certainly as severe as any other churchman about knights killing people other than in that precise context. In the *De laude novae militiae* he has very harsh words for the warrior class and its culture. He is careful to make the point, however, echoing St Augustine — and, as has just been seen, more recently the unknown Hugh the Sinner — that fighting is not in itself evil if the warrior is fighting out of a good intention.

With the theory in place, with a rule of life and rapidly expanding numbers (they were indeed even established near London's Chancery Lane by early 1129, moving to what is now known as The Temple in 1161) what the Templars now needed was approval by the papacy. In 1139 Pope Innocent II issued the foundational bull known, as was customary, from the opening Latin words of the title, as *Omne datum optimum* — "every good gift". This effectively brought them under the protection of the popes. Celestine II published *Milites Templi* ("Knights of the Temple") in 1144, which encouraged Christians to give money to the Order: the Pope promised that donations would bring the donor a remission of a seventh of his penance. The following year *Militia Dei* ("The army of God") of Eugenius III allowed the Templars to own churches and cemeteries, and to earn the fees that were attached to them.

BEQUEST

The most remarkable gift, however, preceded these bulls. At his death in 1134 King

Alfonso I of Aragon, Alfonso the Battler, whose 30-year reign had vastly extended his kingdom at the expense of the Muslims, left the whole of his realm to be divided equally between the priests – the canons – who served the Church of the Holy Sepulchre in Jerusalem, the Templars, and to the "Hospital of the Poor" in Jerusalem. Not surprisingly perhaps, the will was not implemented as Alfonso intended. But eventually it left the Templars well endowed in the Iberian peninsular.

The bequest mentions Jerusalem's "Hospital of the Poor". The hospital had been begun in the middle years of the eleventh century within the Abbey of St Mary of the Latins, a monastery funded and staffed largely by merchants and monks from the city of Amalfi in Italy. Near the abbey a house was established for poor pilgrims. It was in existence by 1080, and it was dedicated to St John because it was on the spot where, it was claimed, the conception of John the Baptist had been announced to his father who was a priest serving the Temple. A confraternity of brothers looked after the pilgrims, following the rule of life attributed to St Augustine. Its first prior, named in a bull of Pope Paschal II of 1113 as its founder, was one Brother Gerard, about whom next to nothing is known, not even his nationality.

Brother Gerard was a practical man. He took advantage of the conquest of the Holy Land by the crusaders to establish new hospitals, or refuges, in Europe to give hospitality to poor pilgrims making their way to Palestine. Most of them were established in coastal towns from which travelers might make their way by sea. To support their charitable activity the Hospitallers were granted lands within the newly established Latin Kingdom of Jerusalem. Gerard died in 1120, after attending the council at Nablus. His epitaph recalls in its last line his success in raising funds.

None of this was activity of a warlike kind, and it is unclear when, and how, the Hospitallers became a military Order. Gerard's successor was a French knight, Raymond du Puy, who must have had rather more sense than had Gerard of the precarious situation in which the Western invaders of Palestine found themselves. By the time of his appointment the Templars had just about come into existence, so the idea of a military Order was known in the Holy Land even if it had not yet received as much ecclesiastical approval as had the charitable work of the Hospitallers. Eventually the Prior of the Hospitallers adopted the title of Master, like the Master of the Templars. That did not happen until about 1140, but other military-style titles, particularly that of "constable", were in use much earlier.

The evidence seems to suggest, therefore, that the Hospitallers became the Knights Hospitallers by a process of assimilation to the Templars. Yet although they were not the first military Order, they were the first to play a significant role in the Holy Land. In 1128 Raymond took part in an expedition against Ascalon. Soon afterwards, in 1136, King Fulk granted the Hospitallers a fortified town of Bethgibelin on the Kingdom's southern frontier: their task was to guard the frontier against attack both directly from Egypt and from Ascalon. Less than a decade later Count Raymond II of Tripoli granted them five castles, one of them the famous Krac de Chevalier on the eastern borders of the Kingdom.

It could be, of course, that the Hospitallers simply employed secular knights to do their fighting for them. That may have been true at first, though it is hardly likely that they would have taken on the maintenance of so enormous a fortress, and so enormous a responsibility, as Krac de Chevaliers had they not been able in some way to man it themselves. Moreover, in 1144 the Count of Tripoli gave an undertaking not to make a truce with the Muslims in the region without the assent of the Hospitallers. That does not sound as if the Hospitallers were simply overlords of the castles without any military commitment. By 1153 there was a requirement that all members of the Hospital of St John of Jerusalem should wear a red cross, as the Templars already did, which suggests that by that time the Order had been militarized.

Certainly it had grown. A new hospital was built to the south of the Church of the Holy Sepulchre. It was vast, with room for 2000 beds, and south of that again, on David Street, were the quarters for the knights and brothers who served the hospital. Raymond du Puy also built a similar hospital, only slightly smaller, at Acre. As the Master of the Temple had done, the Master of the Hospital established throughout Europe a string of overlordships, which brought in money to fund the Hospital, and acted as centers for recruiting knights and brothers.

There were other military Orders created in the Holy Land in the twelfth century. The most important of them was the Teutonic Knights, who will be discussed in a later chapter. But there were still others, founded in imitation of the Hospitallers, such as that of the Order of St Lazarus, for Lepers, which may even have had the same founder – Gerard – as the Hospitallers. The Hospitallers of St Thomas of Acre, an Order which came into being at the end of the twelfth century, had English origins: the "Thomas" of the title is Thomas of Canterbury. At some, undefined, point in their history all these Orders become wholly or in part militarized, whatever their origins. But in practice only the Templars, the Hospitaller Knights of St John and the Teutonic Knights played any significant part in the defense of the Latin Kingdom in the East. It was an enterprise that was doomed to failure.

1. As given in Bainton, *Christian attitudes to war and peace* (Nashville TN: Abingdon Press, 1960), pp. 111–12.

2. As was remarked above, no full account of Urban's sermon survives – all that is given here is the sense of what was said.

3. Peters, F. E., *Jerusalem* (Princeton NJ: Princeton University Press, 1985), p. 286.

Chapter Four

Defense of the Kingdom

After the capture of Jerusalem the paramount need was to establish control of the coast. By 1110 Arsuf, Caesarea, Haifa, Acre, Beirut, and Sidon had been captured. Tyre held out until 1124. Ascalon still held out, which created a serious problem because it served as a base for the Egyptian Fatimids from which they could mount sorties into the southern region of the Kingdom. As has been seen, in 1136 the Hospitallers were given charge of the fortified town of Bethgibelin in an attempt to neutralize the threat from Ascalon, as well as to defend the southern frontier. There was, at first, even further expansion of the crusader kingdom across the Jordan: the newly acquired territory was simply named Outrejourdain – Transjordan.

Though the numbers who had traveled on crusade were relatively large, the numbers who stayed and settled were fairly small. There were at first attempts to drive non-Latins from the Kingdom, but they were soon abandoned on the pragmatic grounds that such people were needed to tend the fields and provide craftsmen and traders. A modus vivendi was reached whether with non-Latin Christians, Muslims or Jews. Indeed, despite the pogroms that had accompanied the first crusaders as they passed through Europe, the Jewish population in Palestine was on the whole well treated, and treated better than in contemporary Europe.

The structures of the crusader states mirrored those in Europe. The count of Edessa, the most exposed of the states, did homage for his overlordship to the King of

Jerusalem, as did the count of Tripoli. Antioch theoretically owed homage to the Emperor in Constantinople, but for the most part had to rely upon the support of the King of Jerusalem.

The first of the Christian states to be established had been that of Edessa. It was also the first to fall. It capitulated on Christmas Eve 1144 to a Muslim army commanded by Imad al-Din Zangi, the Atabeg of Aleppo and Mosul. The capture of

The capture of Acre

Edessa (at first only the city, but the rest of the county, despite being purchased by the Byzantines, was taken by Zangi's son Nur al-Din over the next few years, falling finally in 1169) sent shockwaves westwards to Europe. It is not easy to establish the exact order of events. The news of the Muslim conquest of Edessa must have reached Europe by the spring of 1145, but at first there is no sense that anything urgent had to be done. Then the head of the Armenian Church, the Catholicos, arrived in Italy to meet the Pope. He came at the very end of December of that year, clearly alarmed by the threat to his fellow Christians in the region. But as far as he was concerned the

The cloisters at Le Puy in France — one of the places from which French pilgrims began their journey to Jerusalem

threat came more from the Emperor in Constantinople than the Muslims.

More directly concerned about the fall of Edessa was Bishop Hugh of Jabala in Syria who also turned up at the papal court. He had gone there for his own reasons. These had little to do with the general situation in the Latin Kingdom, but his visit, apart from making the Pope, the Cistercian monk Eugenius III, more aware of the problems in the crusader states, managed to effect a reconciliation between the patriarch of Antioch and the papacy, a rapprochement which further antagonized the Byzantine Emperor.

On 1 December 1145 Eugenius issued the very first crusading bull. Entitled *Quantum praedecessores* ('How much our predecessors', i.e., the popes), it called upon the people of Europe, but especially the nobility, to go on crusade. He mentioned the fall of Edessa: the archbishop, his clergy and many other Christians, have been killed, he said, saints' relics have been scattered and trampled under foot by the infidel. Freedom from harassment over debt — which may well have been a particular attraction — and safety for their families while they were away was promised to anyone who set out for Palestine. They were, however, to take the expedition seriously: no dressing up in fine clothes for the journey, no dogs, and no falcons.

There was, however, an important new element. The Church had long imposed penances on sinners, one of the most serious of the penances being a pilgrimage, especially a pilgrimage to Jerusalem. In 1089 Pope Urban II offered the same spiritual benefits that would be gained through a pilgrimage to Jerusalem to anyone ready to help rebuild the church in Tarragona, which had been destroyed by the Muslims. The spiritual benefits promised by Urban at Clermont in 1095 have already been mentioned. In the first half of the twelfth century theological thinking had moved on, and the doctrine now called "indulgences" had begun to emerge. The Church imposed punishments on sinners, but so did God. What the Church had imposed it could obviously remove, but now the Pope seemed to be saying that the Church could also remove the punishment imposed by God.

Not that Eugenius quite says so expressly in *Quantum praedecessores*, but he goes a good way in that direction, and may very well have been understood to make that claim:

By the authority of omnipotent God and Blessed Peter the Prince of the Apostles, conceded to us by God, we grant remission of and absolution from sins . . . in such a way that whosoever devoutly begins and completes such a holy journey or dies on it will obtain absolution from all his sins concerning which he has made confession with a contrite and humble heart; and he will receive the fruit of everlasting recompense from the rewarder of all. [1]

At a court held at Christmas 1145 in Bourges, Louis VII, the King of France, announced that he would be going on a crusade — though it is not clear whether he had decided to do so after reading *Quantum praedecessores*, or whether he was already personally determined to do so. His barons were not impressed, and for a while it seemed that nothing was going to happen. Eugenius had become a monk at Clairvaux under the influence of Bernard, though Bernard had not been impressed when his former disciple was made Pope, thinking him too inexperienced. Now the Saint wrote to the Pope making suggestions for improving the text of his bull. Eugenius made the changes and, for good measure, appointed Bernard official preacher of the crusade. He reissued a slightly modified version of *Quantum praedecessores* on 1 March 1146

He preached at Vezelay at Easter, on 31 March. He preached out in the open, his hearers crowding into the fields that fall away from the hilltop shrine of Mary Magdalen. King Louis took the cross, and so did so many others that Bernard had to resort to tearing up his clothes to produce makeshift crosses. He then set out on a crusade of his own, preaching not only in France, but in Flanders and in Germany. His message, which he no doubt sincerely believed, was simple, though dressed up in his splendid eloquence: those who took the cross would receive full remission for their sins. At Christmas Bernard was in Speyer where he met the German King Conrad III and persuaded him, too, to depart for the Holy Land. At a meeting in Frankfurt am Main he declared that the German expedition against the pagan Wends was also a crusade, and worthy of the same kind of privileges that had been bestowed on the crusade against the Muslims. A rather reluctant Pope Eugenius, who probably would have preferred Conrad to have been left out of it, and who went to France in 1147 to talk it all over with Bernard, had little option but to agree.

And so the second crusade was launched: the army of the German king leaving at the end of May, that of King Louis a month later. That was the first problem. Both armies followed the same overland route to Constantinople, which meant that when the French went by there were few provisions still left to feed them. The two Western Kings had little friendship towards each other, and neither had any for the Byzantine Emperor Manuel, though Conrad's sister-in-law married him.

The Germans, having arrived first, departed first for Asia Minor. Conrad's force divided in two. One part, consisting of non-combatant pilgrims and led by Bishop Otto of Freising, Conrad's half-brother, made their way directly to Jerusalem. The combatants engaged the Turks at Dorylaeum on 25 October, and were soundly defeated. The surviving Germans now joined the French, though Conrad himself, who had been taken ill, returned to Constantinople to convalesce. He eventually reached Acre by ship the following April.

The Battle of Dorylaeum

The French fared marginally better, but only because of the assistance of the Master of the French Templars. Some 130 Templar knights had met in Paris in April 1146 with the King of France, the Pope, four archbishops and sundry nobles. It is quite probably on that occasion that Eugenius granted the Templars the right to wear their distinctive red cross. The French Master made a great impression on King Louis, and served as his negotiator with the Emperor Manuel. When Louis's army came under attack from the Turks after it had crossed the Bosphorus the King put the Master in charge, and he divided the French army into units, each under the command of a Templar knight. When they reached the coast Louis and the few horses remaining took ship. The remainder of the army struggled on, now less than half its original size.

They regrouped in Antioch, where Louis, now desperately short of funds, had to beg a loan from the Templars. There his Queen, Eleanor of Acquitaine, took the side of her uncle, Raymond, Prince of Antioch, over whether the crusade should, as originally intended, go on to attempt the reconquest of Edessa. But what had begun for Louis as a crusade, he had by this time come to look upon more as a pilgrimage. He was therefore determined to make his way to Jerusalem. Eleanor wanted to stay in the city, but Louis compelled her to continue with him to Jerusalem, leaving Edessa to its fate. In June, however, he was once again reminded of the reason for his journey, and the realities of warfare in the East.

A council met at Acre on 24 June. It was attended by the King of Jerusalem, Baldwin III, the Patriarch of Jerusalem, the Archbishops of Caesarea and Nazareth, and the two Grand Masters — of the Temple and of the Hospital. The decision was taken to attack Damascus. The Templars seem to have been behind this plan which, had it succeeded, would undoubtedly have relieved pressure on the Latin Kingdom by driving a wedge between the Muslims of the Northeast and those of the South. But tactically it was a mistake. Jerusalem and Damascus shared a common enemy, Nur al-Din. An alliance might have been possible, and if so, preferable to an assault which the Christians could not be sure of winning. But it was not to be the last time that the Templars pressed a risky strategy. The more sensible plan would have been to go to the aid of Antioch, hard pressed by Nur al-Din.

The attack on Damascus was a disastrous failure. Instead of dividing the armies of Islam, the assault united them, and left Antioch vulnerable. When Nur al-Din defeated Raymond in 1149, he sent the Prince's head as a trophy to the Caliph in Baghdad.

There were mutual recriminations among the Christians, the Franks of the Kingdom of Jerusalem blaming the crusaders for the failure at Damascus, and vice versa. Conrad and Louis returned to their kingdoms, the crusading ideal tarnished by defeat. The European powers were unwilling to come to the aid of their cousins in the

Levant for a generation. Even the crusade Bernard had declared against the Wends ended in failure. Bernard had called for the infidel nations either to be converted or exterminated. Neither happened, some of the Slavs turning out already to be Christian, others remaining obdurately pagan. Bernard's reputation shrank, and he was plagued by self-doubts.

BATTLE FOR SURVIVAL

In the Kingdom of Jerusalem, however, the battle for survival continued. There were threats on two fronts, from Damascus in the North and from Egypt in the South. To protect the Kingdom against Egypt, the Templars were given charge of Gaza sometime about 1150. It was fortified, and became the Knights' first major castle. It is possible that from the late 1130s they had held a string of castles in the North of which Baghras was the most important. It stood 26 kilometers north of Antioch at the Syrian Gates, the entrance to the Belen Pass, and the Knights renamed it Gaston. But as Malcolm Barber, the historian of the Order, has pointed out, in the 1130s the Templars would have had neither the men nor the money to build castles. They must therefore have taken over already existing fortifications. Gaza, on the other hand, was to be all their own work. The purposes of this grant to the Templars, and of the earlier one to the Hospitallers of Bethgibelin, was to isolate the Egyptian-held port of Ascalon.

Ascalon was besieged in the summer of 1153, both Hospitallers and Templars taking part in the assault. The Christian camp was one night awakened by an uproar. The Templars, having forced a breach in the wall, were fighting their way inside. All non-Templars were held back by the Templar commander. It is not clear why he did this. It may have been to win for the Order the greater part of the booty — as many contemporaries suspected — or it may have been to win for them greater glory. Either way, the result was disastrous. The 40 knights who entered the city were all killed, and their bodies hung over the battlements for everyone to see. At that point, and after a long siege in the heat of the summer, many in the Christian army wanted to abandon the struggle. The Patriarch of Jerusalem, and the Hospitallers, urged them to continue. The town held out just a week longer before surrendering.

A decade later both Hospitallers and Templars were in action as King Amalric took the battle to Egypt itself. In 1164 and again in 1167 there were expeditions even though the Templars' commitment to the Northern frontier, and the loss of 60 knights at Harim in August, meant they were desperately short of men. The outcome was a treaty with the Vizier Shawan. Amalric, however, was dissatisfied. The only way, he believed, to avert the Latin Kingdom being surrounded by a united Islamic state — which Nur-al-Din was attempting to establish — was by annexing Egypt. A further expedition was proposed for 1168.

The Templars objected. The overt reason for their objection was that a treaty had been made with the Vizier, and the Christians were in honor bound to keep it. More cynical commentators have suggested they objected because the Hospitallers were also to take part and, after the division of the booty, would have ended up a military force even more powerful than the Templars. Certainly the motive behind the Hospitallers seems to have been money. They were desperately short of cash. Five hundred Knights Hospitaller joined the October expedition. It ended in disaster as the Caliph in Cairo called upon the aid of Nur-al-Din, thus establishing the alliance that the attack had been intended to prevent. The Master of the Hospital resigned his office.

Amalric's strategy had not only failed but failed spectacularly. In 1173 he attempted an even riskier one. He tried to win over the Islamic sects of the Assassins, who had split from the Egyptian Fatimids, and had settled in the Lebanese mountains — their leader was known to the Franks as "the Old Man of the Mountains". The Assassins sent an ambassador to Jerusalem. On his way home under a safe-conduct the ambassador was set upon by Templars; he was killed by a one-eyed knight called Walter of Mesnil. Amalric was incensed, and had Walter thrown into prison, despite protests from the Templar Grand Master. Templar apologists presented the episode as a response to the disgrace of a Christian king dealing with a Muslim sectary. A more likely explanation is that the Templars wanted to frustrate the alliance because the Assassins paid them tribute, which would have been lost had the King's plan come to fruition.

Amalric may have been misguided, but he was determined. His successors were far less effective. Baldwin IV, who came to the throne in 1174, was a leper. He died childless in 1186, leaving his 8-year-old nephew, also Baldwin, as heir and the Count of Tripoli, Raymond, as regent. Baldwin V died the following year, and the crown was given to Guy de Lusignan. This coup d'etat was engineered by, among others, Gerard de Ridefort, who was Master of the Temple: the Master of the Hospital was bitterly opposed on the grounds that it contravened his oath of loyalty. For the conspirators Gerard's principled stance was problematic because he had possession of the keys to the treasury — where the regalia was kept. Eventually he threw the key out of a window, but refused to attend, or to let any of his knights attend, the coronation of King Guy.

Guy could not afford an enemy as powerful as the Count of Tripoli. The two Grand Masters were sent to effect a reconciliation. They set off towards Tripoli, but en route heard of a party of Muslims who had been allowed by Raymond to cross his territory in compliance with the terms of his treaty with Saladin, Nur al-Din's former general and now successor. The crusader party decided to attack the Muslims. They gathered knights, some 140 in all, of whom half were Templars, and rode to the Springs of Cresson, only to discover that the Muslims numbered some 7,000. The Master of the Hospital advised caution, but was taunted for his cowardice by Guy de Ridefort. They attacked, and were massacred, only the Templar leader and two of his knights escaping the slaughter. The heads of the Christian knights were carried on the lances of the Muslims.

Saladin

The disaster made Raymond realize that his conflict with Guy was too dangerous to maintain, and he was reconciled. But by this time Saladin had gathered a huge army, said to have been some 100,000 men, and crossed the River Jordan just south of Lake Tiberias. He captured the city of Tiberias, though not the citadel where Raymond's wife took refuge. He then camped at Hattin, beside the lake. The crusaders took council at Acre.

On 2 July 1187 the crusading army of some 20,000 foot soldiers and 1,300 knights set up camp just north of Nazareth. There was plenty of grazing for their horses and an ample supply of water for men and beasts. Raymond's advice was that they should stay there until the heat of the summer forced the Muslims to withdraw. He said this, even though his wife was trapped within Tiberias. His advice was accepted, but that night Gerard de Ridefort persuaded King Guy to launch an attack. The army marched forward through treeless, waterless hills. It arrived parched and weary above Lake Tiberias where Guy ordered them to camp for the night: the Templars had said they could go no further though the parched soldiers wanted to reach the lake.

The following morning the Christian army awoke to find themselves surrounded. Raymond was allowed to escape, but the Christian army was otherwise almost entirely destroyed. All Templar and Hospitaller prisoners were executed on Saladin's orders. According to the Arab chronicler Ibn al-Athir, Saladin bought all the Templars and Hospitallers from their captors at 50 Egyptians dinars each.

> Immediately he got two hundred prisoners who were decapitated at his command. He had these particular men killed because they were the fiercest of all the Frankish warriors, and in this way he rid the Muslim people of them. He sent an order to Damascus to kill all those [Templars and Hospitallers] found in his territory, whoever they belonged to, and this was done. [2]

Only Gerard de Ridefort was spared, buying his release by ordering the Templars to surrender Gaza. It was an ignominious end, made all the worse by the loss of the relic of the True Cross which had been taken into battle as a talisman. The defeat at the Horns of Hattin – so called from the two-peaked hill on which Guy made his last

Ajlun Castle, Jordan overlooks the Jordan Valley. It was built by the Arabs against the Crusaders, AD 1184-1214

Inside Ajlun Castle

stand – led to the loss of almost all the Latin Kingdom, Jerusalem itself falling to Saladin on 2 October. The city of Tyre survived only because of the chance arrival there by sea of a crusading force under Conrad of Montferrat. Antioch and Tripoli also remained in Christian hands, though both with loss of territory. The remnant of the Hospitallers fell back to their castle of Belvoir, but after a siege of eighteen months that, too, was surrendered. Their headquarters was from then on at the castle of Margat in Tripoli.

The shock of the fall of Jerusalem was enormous. Pope Urban III was said to have died of it. His successor Gregory VIII only ruled as pope for two months, but had issued a new call for a crusade even before he was crowned as pontiff. Response was swift, despite a confused situation within Europe itself. The first to commit himself was Richard of Poitou who was, shortly afterwards, to become King Richard

Richard and Saladin jousting

I of England. Philip II (Philip Augustus) of France followed suit, and after him the German Emperor Frederick Barbarossa. Frederick was the first to set out, leaving Regensburg on I May 1189; the English and French kings set off together from Vezelay on 4 July the following year. Frederick took the land route, Philip and Richard going by sea – Richard stopping off at Cyprus, to wrest it from its Byzantine ruler, an action which was later to have important consequences.

Frederick's army spent the winter near Constantinople, crossing the Bosphorus in the spring of 1190. It was a long and difficult march and then, on 10 June, Frederick accidentally drowned as he was crossing the river Saleph (Göksu). His army disintegrated; some went home, others took ship to the Holy Land, and others again under the command of Frederick's son, Duke Frederick, continued by land to Antioch – where Duke Frederick also died.

Philip and Richard arrived at Acre in April and June 1191 respectively. Acre fell to the crusaders the following July, at which point Philip, claiming he had completed his crusading vow, returned home (via Rome to get absolution from the Pope, just in case the vow had not after all been fulfilled). Richard, on the other hand, marched south towards Jaffa, defeating Saladin at the battle of Arsuf on 7 September, where the Templars held the front rank, and the Hospitallers the rear. Which was exactly the opposite of how they marched under Richard's command – the Hospitallers in the rear, the Templars in the van. Three days later the crusaders reached Jaffa.

The goal of the crusade was, of course, the liberation of Jerusalem. Twice – in

January 1192 and again the following June – Richard was in sight of the city, but he was advised that to capture and hold it was beyond the means of his troops, and he withdrew. Meanwhile he rebuilt Ascalon as a defense against Saladin's armies. In August Saladin attempted to recapture Jaffa, but failed, and an armistice was reached in September. According to it, the Christians were to be left in control of the coastal strip between Acre and Jaffa, pilgrims were to have access to Jerusalem – and the defenses of Ascalon were to be demolished. Richard departed Palestine in October, but not before selling Cyprus to Guy de Lusignan. Guy had been deposed as King of Jerusalem; the title was now held by Conrad of Montferrat. Guy was Richard's second choice for Cyprus. He had first made it over to the Templars who sent a small force of 20 to occupy it, but their behavior – and their efforts to raise taxes – alienated the inhabitants. Under Guy and his successors as Latin kings of Cyprus the Templars continued to garrison several castles on the island.

Instead of Jerusalem Acre was now the capital of the Kingdom of Jerusalem. The Templars moved their headquarters there. The Hospitallers had an immense hospital in Acre, and the city's biggest church, and they, too, eventually moved their headquarters there, though for some years they maintained them at their castle of Margat. Relations between the two Orders was at least civil, though there were squabbles – once over the use of ovens. But by now the Templars were facing criticism across Europe, in particular over their claims on church revenues such as tithes. The Pope at the turn of the twelfth and thirteen centuries, Innocent III, was not unaware of such complaints, but while condemning the Templars for their pride, was ready to support them in their demands for funds. Pope Innocent wanted another crusade.

When it came it was a disaster, though not for the usual reasons. The Pope declared a crusade in August 1198. He also wrote a letter to the Emperor in Constantinople, criticizing the Greeks not only for their failure to submit to Rome, but also because they did not aid the Christians in the Holy Land. Innocent appealed both for Christian unity, and for assistance for the crusader states. Meanwhile the crusade was preached in France and Germany. A substantial army was gathered, with the intention of attacking Egypt, thus making the Christian hold on Palestine, such as it was, more secure. The Venetians contracted to provide transport.

By October 1202 only a third of the army had reached Venice, and they could not raise the money the Venetians demanded for their transport onwards. In return for the services of the Venetians, therefore, they undertook to assist them in recovering a city on the Dalmatian coast, which they did, despite Innocent's prohibition against their attacking other Christians.

There were further complications when the leaders of the crusade (it is formally called the fourth crusade, though the numbering really bears very little relation to the various expeditions to the Holy Land after the first one) became embroiled in the dynastic struggles in Constantinople itself, which led to the Christian capital being attacked and occupied on 17 July 1203. Alexius IV, who had undertaken

The church of Santa Sophia, Istanbul

Baldwin of Flanders dispenses justice to a miscreant

to try to re-establish union between the Greek and the Latin Church, was crowned as co-emperor with his father in the church of Hagia Sophia on 1 August.

But there was much unrest in the city, partly because of the unpopular efforts to reunite the Churches, partly because of the presence of the crusaders. There was a palace coup, and Alexius IV and his father were assassinated. The new Emperor, Alexius V, was opposed to the crusaders, and was therefore overthrown. Between 12 and 15 April the ancient city was pillaged by the crusaders, abetted by the Venetians. "Even the Muslims would have been more merciful," wrote a Greek chronicler. Count Baldwin of Flanders became Emperor, a Latin prelate the Patriarch. Byzantine territory was taken over, and divided among the Western barons. The Pope himself was furious, but his legate with the crusaders dispensed them from their crusading vow so long as they remained in the new Latin Empire for two years.

The Byzantines recovered the city in 1261, but in between times the maintenance of the Latin Empire in Constantinople was a drain on Western resources which might otherwise have been employed in defense of the Holy Land. Immediately, however, the Sultan of Egypt, terrified by the barbarity the crusaders had displayed in Constantinople, sued for peace, and a ten-year armistice was agreed between himself and the Kingdom of Jerusalem.

Pope Innocent was not content with the truce, or with the failure of his crusade. He proclaimed another in 1208, but his appeal went unanswered. When he summoned the Fourth Lateran Council to meet in Rome in November 1215, the bull calling it together insisted that one of its purposes was to bring peace, so that Christians would be free to go on crusade. And immediately after Innocent's opening sermon after the Council had met, the Patriarch of Jerusalem appealed for help for the Holy Land. When its canons were drawn up, number 71 began, "It is our ardent desire to liberate the Holy Land from infidel hands," and it went on to lay down the time and place for the crusaders going by sea to gather – either at Brindisi or Messina – on 1 June 1217. Those going by the land route were to be ready by the same date. The canon dealt with the spiritual, as well as the physical, preparedness of those going on the crusade, and extended the promise of remission of sins not just to those who went or provided transport, but even to those who built the ships which would carry the army. There was to be no shipping to the East, both so that accommodation would be available for the crusaders, and so the Saracens would be deprived of it. Prelates were to preach the crusade, and a tax was to be levied to pay for it – Innocent's own contribution was in the hands of the Latin Patriarch, and the Grand Masters of the Temple and the Hospital. Indeed, although the canon did not say so, all money gathered for the crusade was channeled through the Templar treasury in Paris.

In July 1217 Pope Innocent's successor, Honorius III, wrote to the two Grand Masters and to the Latin Patriarch of Jerusalem, to meet King Andrew of Hungary and Duke Leopold of Austria on the island of Cyprus. The meeting never happened, but the King and the Duke made their way with their armies to Acre and there, in October 1217, they decided to attack Egypt. The winter was spent in small-scale expeditions against Muslims, and in January King Andrew returned home while King Frederick II of Germany, who in 1215 had undertaken to go on a crusade, never turned up.

But the attack on Egypt went ahead. It began in May 1218 with the Templars very much to the fore, building bridges across the canals, which barred the way of the invaders. It was not until November the following year that their first objective, the town of Damietta at the entrance to the River Nile, was captured. The Sultan of Egypt sued for peace. He offered to surrender the entire Kingdom of Jerusalem apart from the region east of the River Jordan, in return for Damietta. He had indeed made the offer before the city was taken, but it had been haughtily rejected by the papal representative, Cardinal Pelagius, though John de Brienne, the King of Jerusalem, was in favor.

The Templars tended at first to sympathize with Pelagius, believing that Jerusalem was too difficult to defend without its hinterland, but as time went on they began to have second thoughts, doubts sown by the harrying of Christian lands in Palestine by the ruler of Damascus. In June 1221 the peace offer was made once more, but still Pelagius stood out against it. He was expecting the arrival of Frederick II – the Pope had crowned him Emperor in 1220 to encourage him on his way. By this time the Templars were definitely in favor of the terms offered. Nonetheless the crusaders pressed on southwards. It was a mistake. The Egyptians opened sluice gates, filled canals, and cut off the crusaders' retreat. This time there was little argument. The crusaders withdrew from Egypt after an exchange of prisoners.

THE EXCOMMUNICATED EMPEROR

In 1225 the Emperor Frederick married the daughter, and heir, of John de Brienne. He still put off going on the crusade, nevertheless agreeing he might be excommunicated had he not launched his crusade by 1227. When, in 1227, he fell ill and once again delayed his departure for the Holy Land, Honorius' successor, Pope Gregory IX, duly excommunicated the Emperor. Consequently when he at last arrived in Palestine, though he was given a generous welcome, as an excommunicate he was treated with considerable caution. When, in November 1228, he marched from Acre down to Jaffa the military Orders did not march with him, but followed on a day behind.

Pope Gregory IX

There may have been reasons other than the excommunication to account for the simmering hostility to the Emperor. His activities in Italy had driven a number of barons off their lands, and some had joined the Templars. He was also German, and thought to be too close to the Teutonic knights – he once asked the Templars to hand over a fortress to a garrison of Germans, and was rebuffed.

But when Frederick arrived he had the considerable advantage that the Sultan of Egypt was very weak, and not ready to defend his territory. The Sultan offered a ten-year truce and the return of Jerusalem to the Christians. There were conditions. Jerusalem was to remain unfortified and the Temple area itself was to be under the control of Muslims. And during the truce the fortifications of castles held by the Templars and the Hospitallers were not to be improved. Not surprisingly the Knights were unimpressed by these terms, as was the Latin Patriarch: they were conscious of the problem of holding Jerusalem without control of the surrounding territory. Frederick, however, agreed to the proposals. He stayed two nights in Jerusalem, and despite his excommunication wore his crown in the church of the Holy Sepulchre. The Patriarch put the city under an interdict.

The Knights gathered at Acre; Frederick's truce, they pointed out, did not cover Damascus, and they must expect attack from that quarter. Frederick was furious. He held an assembly in the open air during which he fiercely attacked the military Orders, and even went on to besiege the Templar headquarters in

Church of the Holy Sepulchre

Acre. Then he sailed away, only to send, two years later, a force under Ricardo Filangieri. Filangieri was to act as Frederick's representative in the Holy Land, but the leading nobles would not accept him in that capacity, and his authority was confined to Tyre where he resided.

In 1241, however, Filangieri was secretly admitted into Acre through a gate under the control of the Hospitallers, and with him the Hospitallers plotted to reassert the authority of the King – whose representative Filangieri was – against the nobles. The conspiracy was discovered, and from October 1241 to the following March the residence of the treacherous Hospitallers was besieged by, among others, the Templars. The Hospitaller Grand Master marched to its relief from his headquarters at Margat. Agreement was eventually reached, which included the surrendering of Tyre to the nobles, and peace was restored, but it had been one of the more significant clashes between the two main military Orders in the Holy Land. Otherwise there was a good deal of collaboration. In 1233, for example, when the Sultan of Hamah refused to pay the expected tribute to the Hospitallers, the Templars joined with Hospitallers in forcing him to do so.

SUMMONS TO A CRUSADE

Matters began to become more complicated in the late 1230s. The truce with Egypt negotiated by Frederick was to expire in 1239. The Pope sent out another summons to a crusade; the most distinguished person to respond was Theobald, King of Navarre and Count of Champagne. He arrived in the Holy Land on 1 September 1239, at a moment when the Muslim leadership was in some confusion. Theobald decided to attack the Egyptians, but an expedition against Gaza ended in disaster – and the Templars and Hospitallers were blamed for not supporting it.

The came a surprising breakthrough for the Franks. The Sultan of Damascus decided he needed their support against the Sultan of Cairo, and in the middle of 1240 agreed to hand back the Transjordanian territories, as well as returning the castle of Safad to the Templars, in return for crusader support against Egypt. Theobald, however, was no longer eager to attack Egypt, possibly because of prisoners held there since the defeat at Gaza. He left the Holy Land in September 1240.

There was now a major disagreement, which fed into the conflict over Filangieri mentioned above. The Hospitallers were in favor of a deal with Egypt; the Templars, who had been behind the treaty with Damascus, were opposed to such a course of action. They also supported Richard of Cornwall who came on a crusade just as Theobald left, and stayed until the following May, organizing the release of the prisoners held by the Egyptians. Richard, who was the Emperor Frederick's brother-in-law, was naturally a supporter of the imperialist policy, hence Hospitaller support for Frederick's representative Filangieri. It was wasted effort: the Emperor's force in Tyre was driven out of the city in 1243 by the Christian nobility of the Kingdom of Jerusalem.

Templar, rather than Hospitaller, policy won the day after Richard returned home. The treaty with the Sultan of Damascus was revived, and almost all lands west of the Jordan were handed back to the Christians. Even the Temple area came back into Christian hands, contrary to the treaty with Egypt that Frederick had made. The Emperor was furious, and threatened to seize all Templar lands in the areas of Europe he governed.

King Louis IX disembarking from his ship

The Sultan of Egypt, feeling himself extremely vulnerable against the combined forces of Damascus and the Kingdom of Jerusalem, now sought the assistance of the Khorezmian Turks, whose center was near Edessa. The Turks marched south and on 11 July 1244 sacked Jerusalem. The Christian forces, reunited against this latest threat, at first felt themselves too weak to defend the city. But they finally faced the Turks at La Forbie (Harbiyah) on 17 October. Like the Horns of Hattin, it was a complete disaster. Only 33 Templars, 26 Hospitallers, and three Teutonic Knights survived. The Grand Master of the Temple just disappeared. It was presumed he was taken prisoner: the Sultan refused even to consider a ransom.

In the December of that year King Louis IX of France, who was afterwards declared a saint, took his crusading vows. He did not rush into action. His crusade, which is estimated to have cost some six times the annual income of the French crown, was prepared with great care, not just the recruitment of men, but the hiring of ships. When the force finally set out in August 1248 most of the troops and their leaders came from French crown lands, though there were groups from Italy, Scotland, and some 200 knights from England.

Louis arrived at Limassol on 17 September and spent the winter in Cyprus while waiting for other contingents to arrive. He had to warn the Master of the Temple that he could not pursue the common Templar policy of negotiating with the Muslims.

The crusaders' plan was to attack Egypt. They landed there on 5 June 1249, and took Damietta the following day. They then advanced slowly towards Cairo, the Templar knights in the lead. On 5 February 1250 part of the force crossed a branch of the Nile in front of the town of Mansurah. The story of what happened next is confused. One possible account is that in his eagerness for military glory the Count of Anjou rushed forward towards the town, and the Templars, not to be outdone, did likewise. What is certain is that the Christians were trapped in Mansurah's narrow streets and massacred: some 280 Templars died including, in the fighting that followed, their Grand Master.

With the Hospitallers and the Templars providing the rearguard, Louis was forced to retreat. Again, during the retreat many died, and Louis himself was

The Crusaders' attack on Damietta

captured. To gain his freedom he was required to hand back Damietta and pay a very large ransom. He was unable to raise the sum from his own resources, and approached the Templars for a loan. The Templars' treasury was on board one of the galleys which had transported them to Egypt. Their treasurer refused to hand over the money to Louis' emissary, claiming that to do so was contrary to his sworn obligations to the money's donors. The Templar Marshal – the Master having been killed – told the emissary to take the money by force, so that the treasurer would not be obliged to break his oath. This was done, and Louis was released to go back to Acre. He ensured that the new Master would be one who would be on the side of the French King. This at least he achieved: the man elected had been a senior officer of the Order in France, and had been employed by Louis to arrange the transport for his army.

Louis remained in the Holy Land until April 1254, effectively running what was left of the Kingdom. In 1251 the Old Man of the Mountain tried to negotiate.

Louis, he demanded, should either pay him a tribute in return for his life, or the King should agree to cancel the tribute that the Assassin leader had to pay to the Hospitallers and Templars. In the presence of the two Grand Masters Louis rejected the demand. It did not matter whom he killed, he told the Old Man's emissaries, the Orders would survive because they were undying corporations.

SURRENDER OF THE TEMPLARS' POSSESSIONS

The following year Louis discovered that the Templars had been trying to negotiate a separate peace with the Sultan of Damascus in return for some of their lands which had been taken. The King was incensed at these negotiations going on behind his back. He was in any case not eager to make peace with Damascus while the Sultan of Cairo held so many of his force prisoners in Egypt. Louis summoned all the Templars and made them kneel before him to ask forgiveness — and formally to surrender to him all their possessions.

Louis's firm rule gave direction to the remnant of the Kingdom, and he saw to it that the castles of the military Orders — only the Orders were strong enough to build, equipment and maintain the castles — were strengthened against future attack, as well as other fortifications. But soon after he had left a minor civil war took place in the Holy Land between two of the major trading powers, the Venetians and the Genovese, with the Templars and the Teutonic Knights backing the Venetians, and the Hospitallers the Genovese. The small state could not afford such squabbles, and in October 1258 a treaty was finally drawn up regulating the relations between the military Orders.

The threat was now neither Damascus nor Cairo, but the Mongols, who had arrived from Central Asia demanding that the Hospitallers and the Templars recognize their sovereignty. Aleppo and Damascus had fallen to the Mongols, and the Christian Prince of Antioch and the King of Armenia had attempted to buy off trouble by entering treaties with them. Cairo, however, decided to go on the offensive. The Sultan asked for free passage through Christian-held territory, which was given, and assistance from the military orders to defeat the Mongols, which was refused. This was, perhaps, a mistaken decision which might have bought the Christians more time, for the

Egyptian Mamluks (cf. above, p. 49) defeated the Mongols on 3 September 1260 in a major battle just South of Nazareth.

THE ARRIVAL OF PRINCE EDWARD

Early in 1263 the Latin Kingdom opened negotiations with the Mamluk Sultan, and an exchange of prisoners was agreed upon – but the Hospitallers and Templars refused to free their Muslim captives, whose skill as craftsmen was proving profitable to the Orders. The Sultan then advanced on Acre. There was a flurry of letters between the Latin Kingdom and Europe, but to little effect, though King Louis arranged for funds to be made available through the Templar banking system to the Masters of the Hospital and the Temple. Louis indeed launched another crusade, but in 1270 directed it against Tunis where many, including the French King himself, were taken ill and died. The English Prince Edward, who had been part of this expedition now turned towards the Holy Land, arriving there in May 1271.

He arrived not a moment too soon. Castle after castle was falling to the Egyptians. Antioch itself had been taken in May 1266, while the last crusader castle which lay inland, one belonging to the Teutonic Knights, fell in June 1271. Edward's arrival, though he stayed less than 18 months, brought a degree of peace. The Sultan of Egypt agreed a ten-year truce in 1272. The Orders returned to squabbling – over the succession to the Kingdom and succession to the County of Tripoli, the Hospitallers (and Teutonic Knights) backing one candidate, the Templars another.

The Sultanate of Egypt did not abide by the truce. Now the Sultan's objective was to seize the remaining possessions of the Christians along the coastal strip – all that remained of the Latin Kingdom of Jerusalem. The Hospitallers' headquarters at the castle of Margat fell in 1285, and the Egyptians moved against Tripoli. The Templar Master had an informant in the Egyptian army. He knew the attack was coming, and tried to warn Tripoli, but he was not believed.

In August 1290 reinforcements arrived in Acre from Europe. The newcomers, unused to the modus vivendi which prevailed in the Holy Land among those of different faiths – indeed, they were scandalized by it – slaughtered Muslims in the city and surrounding countryside. This was something new, and the Sultan of Cairo demanded reparations. The Templar Master proposed handing over the Christians they had imprisoned; the Hospitallers and Teutonic Knights demurred, arguing that they should explain to the Sultan that the atrocities had been carried out by newcomers who did not understand the customs of the country. Unappeased, the Sultan prepared to attack. Again the Templar Grand Master was warned of the impending assault, but he was not trusted because of Templar links to Muslims, and his information was ignored. When the Templars tried to negotiate with Cairo their emissaries were thrown into goal.

On 5 April 1291 the Mamluk army arrived outside Acre. There were some 160,000 foot soldiers and 60,000 mounted troops. There was an array of siege engines. Inside the city were some 50,000 people, two-thirds of them civilians. All the military Orders were present with their Masters, those of St Lazarus and Thomas of Acre as well as the Teutonic Knights, the Templars and the Hospitallers. There were in all 800 knights and some 14,000 foot soldiers.

On 15 May the Muslim forces crossed the outer wall. The final assault began just before dawn on 18 May, to the sound of Egyptian drums. Terrified civilians made for the quay. A renegade Templar seized one of his Order's ships, and charged heavily for letting refugees aboard; he financed a subsequent military career outside the Order. But there was a storm, and there were too few ships. As they waited in vain on the quay many Christians were butchered by the Egyptians. All the Teutonic knights (except their Grand Master), all the knights of St Thomas of Acre and of St Lazarus died. The Templar fortress within the city held out for a time. Its Marshal negotiated surrender terms, but when the Muslim soldiers entered they started raping and pillaging the refugees who were huddled inside. The Marshal hoisted once more the Templars' black-and-white banner, and returned to the attack.

That night the Templars' treasure, relics, and some of the refugees were sent away by boat to Sidon. The following morning the Sultan again offered terms. When the Marshal went out to negotiate he was beheaded. The siege lasted until 28 May. Mines under the walls caused them to collapse, and the Muslim troops rushed in, but the whole building then collapsed upon them, and upon the Templars still fighting inside.

It was the end of two centuries of crusader presence in the Holy Land. A number of Templar strongholds still remained, but one by one they were abandoned, the last, Atlit, on 14 August 1291. It was impregnable, but useless.

Surviving knights withdrew to Cyprus. The smaller military Orders had effectively been wiped out, the Teutonic Knights had a mission elsewhere, as will be seen. The Hospitallers were to reinvent themselves, and have survived to this day. But for the Templars, after the fall of Acre the end was to soon to come.

---

1. Quoted in Riley-Smith, J., *What were the crusades?* (London, Macmillan, 1977), p. 60.

2. Peters, F. E., *Jerusalem* (Princeton NJ: Princeton University Press, 1985), p. 343.

Chapter Five

Northern Frontier

This is not a book about crusades as such, but about the role of the military Orders. There were many crusades or "holy wars" to which were attached the privileges mentioned in Pope Eugenius's bull *Quantum praedecessores* but in which the Orders were not at all, or only marginally, involved. They were not always directed against Muslims. There were, for instance, crusades against papal opponents in Italy. But perhaps the most notorious of the crusades launched against non-Muslims was that against the Cathars, or Albigensians — so called after the city of Albi in southwest France, which was regarded, in fact somewhat mistakenly, as the center of the movement.

The Cathars were regarded by the Church authorities as Christian heretics, but there was very little that was Christian about their beliefs. Central to their faith was a conviction that there were two Gods, equal and opposite, one of good and one of evil. The evil God had created matter, inside which the spirit, created by the good God, was imprisoned. It was the task of believers, therefore, to free the spirit from the (evil) matter.

Pope Innocent III became seriously alarmed by the spread of the heresy, particularly after his legate, Peter of Castelnau, was murdered by a vassal of Raymond VI, Count of Toulouse. A crusade was proclaimed in 1209, which pitted Raymond of Toulouse and Raymond-Roger, Viscount of Béziers and Carcassonne, against Simon

de Montfort, lord of Montfort-l'Amaury and Epernon, and also heir to the earldom of Leicester – to which his son, also called Simon, eventually managed to succeed.

Simon the elder was killed at the siege of Toulouse in 1218, but the particularly brutal campaign against the Cathars dragged on until 1229. There was, however, another kind of campaign also being waged, that of preaching, and its chief protagonist was the Spaniard Dominic Guzmán.

Dominic was born about the year 1170 at Calaruega in Castile. He became a priest in the cathedral chapter at Osma, and when Alfonso IX, King of Castile, sent the Bishop of Osma to Denmark on a diplomatic mission, Dominic went too. On their way they passed through Toulouse, and encountered Catharism at first hand. Dominic and his Bishop went on to Denmark, but on their return, instead of going straight back to Osma they went to Rome, to ask permission to be allowed to became missionaries to the pagan Cumans in what is now Russia. Pope Innocent rejected their request, insisting that they should work closer to home. They went to the abbey of Citeaux, whose monks had been appointed official preachers against the Cathars, then on to Montpellier where they met the abbot of Citeaux, Peter of Castelnau, and others. The Bishop finally went back to his diocese, but Dominic stayed, founding the Order of Preachers, or Dominicans as they are more usually called, to combat the growth of the heresy alongside military efforts to do likewise: Dominic was close to Simon de Montfort.

As will be seen shortly, the Dominicans were to be active in preaching crusades, especially the crusade against the pagan tribes of northern Europe, but in the context in which they were conceived, it is no surprise that the next major development in the Christian concept of war should have come from the pen of a Dominican friar.

Friar Thomas was born about 1225 near the town of Aquino in Italy – hence his name, Thomas Aquinas. He

St Dominic

Opposite: A ceiling in Albi Cathedral, France

studied in Cologne and in the 1250s taught at the University of Paris, returning there in 1269 and staying there until the end of his life, though when he died in 1274 he was on his way to the Council summoned to meet in Lyons by Pope Gregory X. In 1266 or thereabouts he began his most famous work, a handbook of theology, the *Summa Theologiae*. Though still unfinished at his death, it is in three massive volumes, the second volume being divided into two parts, traditionally known as the "First Part of the Second Part", and the "Second Part of the Second Part". Thomas's treatment of war occurs in the latter, the Second of the Second (abbreviated as IIa IIae) at Question 40.

There are four parts, or "articles", to Question 40, each presenting a problem and answering it in the form common among medieval theologians – giving the arguments for the view opposed to that of the author, then systematically answering them. In the first article Thomas asks whether it is always a sin to wage war. He presents the arguments that it is always a sin – and then refutes these in turn. There are, he says, three conditions required, but if they are present then a war is just.

The first condition is that war must always be declared by the prince (that is, by the lawful authority). No private person, he says, has any business declaring war: he has other means to right injustices. Secondly, Thomas continues, war must be fought for a just cause: those attacked may be attacked only because of some wrong they have done. Finally, a war may only be waged to promote good and avoid evil: there must, that is to say, be a right intention.

In the second article Thomas wonders whether the clergy can fight in wars. They cannot, he says very firmly. In the third article he questions, rather oddly, whether subterfuge may be used in war. Not surprisingly he decides that it can. And finally he revisits the issue of when one may fight, asking whether it is lawful to fight on feast days. As we have seen, the Truce of God movement laid down limitations on which days battle might be joined. Thomas is unsympathetic to that point of view, arguing that no one would suggest there were days when a doctor would not come to heal a patient, so there should not be days when action may not be taken to heal the body politic.

None of this, however, suggests that the heathen can, or ought to, be converted by military force – which is what, in Prussia, the Teutonic Knights set out to do. Indeed, in the thirteenth century the weight of scholarly opinion was against them.

By the time Thomas wrote the *Summa* his Dominican brethren were deeply involved as recruiting agents for the Teutonic Knights. Like the Hospitallers, the Teutonic Knights developed out of a hospice for the sick. In this instance it was at Acre, though the formal, Latin, title of the Order was "hospital of the Germans of Holy Mary in Jerusalem", putting it, by its claim to Jerusalem, on an equal footing with the Hospitallers and the Templars. The hospice at Acre was founded in 1190 by crusaders from Bremen and, perhaps, from Lübeck. Like the Hospitallers, the original members were not knights – or at least not fighting men: the head of it may even have been a priest. It was in that form that, in 1191, it was taken under the protection of the Pope.

In 1198 it developed into a military Order, and as such it was confirmed by Pope Innocent III

Pope Innocent III with St Francis of Assisi

who rather oddly bestowed on it not one but two rules of life – that of the Templars for the military wing, and that of the Hospitallers for those who continued to serve the sick. In place of a priest, a knight became its head, and a succession of privileges made it equal in status to the two older Orders. In the thirteenth century it fought in the Holy Land alongside the Templars and the Hospitallers, and controlled a number of castles, mainly around Acre: the Castle of Montfort, in the hills northwest of Acre, was its headquarters.

All the military Orders in the Holy Land were lords of territories across Europe from which they could launch recruiting drives and, perhaps more importantly, gain funds to pay the vast expenses of their presence in Palestine. But the ambitions of the Teutonic Knights were rather wider. They were, for one thing, torn between loyalty to the German Emperors who had been their patrons, donating many of the lordships they held, and loyalty to the papacy. The latter, according to Church law, should have taken precedence, but that did not always happen, particularly when, as was frequently the case, Pope and Emperor were at loggerheads. A Grand Master who, in the middle of the thirteenth century, displayed too much sympathy for the papacy at the expense of the Emperor was forced to resign his office. Eight years later, in 1249, two Grand Masters were elected, one pro-papacy, the other pro-Empire, and it was the imperial candidate who emerged as the victor. The Grand Master was, after all, a prince of the Empire, elevated to that position by the Emperor Frederick II.

Given such strong links with the Empire, it is not surprising the Order looked for crusades within Europe. In 1211 the King of Hungary, Andrew II, gave it Burzenland, fronting the pagan Cumans whom Dominic and his Bishop had wished to convert. But despite having built five forts in the territory it was expelled in 1225 because, the King surmised and probably correctly, it was plotting to undermine his authority in that region, and establish itself as independent.

That such was the Order's intention can be gathered from what happened next. A Polish Duke, Conrad of Masovia, invited it to subdue the pagan Prussians who were harrying his lands. Conrad had led an attack on the Prussians in 1222–1223, but his real interest was in establishing himself as the premier noble in Poland: the Prussians were a distraction which he was only too ready to hand over to the Teutonic Knights.

Efforts to convert the tribes inhabiting the land along the Baltic had begun again in earnest in the 1190s. It was in the hands of German lords and, in particular, of the Archbishop of Bremen, Hartwig II, and his nephew Albert who was Bishop of Riga. Albert was trying to convert Livonia, an area roughly corresponding to the modern Latvia. The Livs, however, made unsatisfactory Christians, reverting to paganism rather too readily when harried by their pagan neighbors. What he needed, decided Albert, was a group of knights who would man a permanent garrison in Livonia, and provide security for his clergy. About 1202 the "Sword Brethren" came into existence, a small military Order – there were probably never more than 180 of them – which was modeled on the Teutonic Knights. The Sword Brethren, or the Brotherhood of the Knighthood of Christ in Livonia as they were more properly known, followed the rule of the Teutonic Knights, and even dressed like them in a white cape, though with a red sword and a small cross on their left shoulders.

The creation of the Sword Brethren led to the establishment of a similar, though still smaller, knighthood for Prussian territories. Again it was a prelate, Bishop Christian, who was the instigator, recruiting a group of northern German knights to defend the small inroads he had made among the Prussians. These knights were given the castle of Dobrzyn on the Vistula as their headquarters, and were generally known as the Knights of Dobrzyn, or Dobrin, in German, though the title they used from c. 1222 was The Knighthood of Christ in Livonia against the Prussians.

However much they might imitate the Teutonic Knights they were very much poor relations, with little independence (both the Sword Brethren and the Knights of Dobrzyn remained tied to their founding bishops though not always happily), and small income. By an agreement of 1204 the Sword Brethren were allowed to retain a third of all the territory they subjugated, the remainder to be handed over to the bishop. The region in which they were active, however, was not only hostile to the knights but unprofitable as well. These knights were, therefore, engaged in a very different form of crusade than the Orders in the Holy Land. They were not trying to regain for Christendom the shrines lost to the infidel, but in the even more dubious activity of supporting by their swords a campaign of evangelization.

Not that the campaign was making much headway. In Livonia the Sword Brethren proved extremely unpopular because of the ruthless way in which they exploited the population – a course forced on them by their lack of finance from other sources. Finance was of the utmost importance, because the number of knights was too small for the task assigned it, and they had to hire, and pay, mercenary troops. "You do not fear to impede the teaching of Christ, provided that you can increase your possessions and revenues," complained Innocent III of the Sword Brethren in 1213.[1]

They developed a distinctly unsavory reputation, not least after the first Master was axed to death by one of the brothers. It was not unknown for them to make war even against Christians for their own gain. They attempted, for instance, to seize lands in Estonia belonging to the King of Denmark – though the papal legate insisted on their giving them back. When a suit was taken out against them in the papal court, the Master decided that he would attempt some kind of amalgamation with the Teutonic Knights who, as will be seen, were already operating in the area, but after an investigation the Teutonic Knights would have nothing more to do with them. In 1236, however, the Sword Brethren were defeated in battle at Saule by the pagan Lithuanians, and some 50 were killed, including the Master. The remainder were taken into the Teutonic Knights the following year.

PAPAL GUARANTEE

Conrad of Masovia had first approached the Teutonic Knights for assistance early in the 1220s, offering them Culmerland more or less as a private fiefdom: in 1226 the Emperor Frederick II made the Grand Master an Imperial Prince for Culmerland and Prussia, which undoubtedly added to the attraction of crusading in the Baltic. A small group of knights made their way to Prussia in 1228, but the Order was still deeply involved in the crusade in the Holy Land, as well as being torn between Pope and Emperor. In 1230 Pope and Emperor settled their differences, the Grand Master of the Knights acting as the Emperor's chief negotiator. Shortly afterwards the Pope guaranteed the right of the Knights to retain all the territories they conquered. Within a week Dominicans in northern Germany were being instructed by the Pope to preach a crusade, recruiting knights to fight for Christ alongside the Teutonic Knights. At first the Dominicans were allowed only to recruit in dioceses neighboring Prussia for knights to fight in Prussia. But the privilege was gradually extended geographically, and knights were allowed to commute their vow to go on crusade in the Holy Land for the crusade in Prussia. Eventually, that, too, was extended, so the Dominicans were allowed to recruit knights to fight also in Livonia.

For the first 40 or so years the preaching of this crusade was limited to the Dominicans. There was to be no deviation from the effort to send men and money via the Teutonic Knights exclusively (as they had early absorbed the Knights of Dobrzyn so they were to do, slightly later, the Sword Brethren) so as not to dissipate energies. Only in the 1260s was the preaching crusade extended to religious Orders other than the Dominicans.

The Teutonic Knights started their Prussian crusade from the Polish fort of Chelmno, or Culm, from which Culmerland took its name. In 1231 the knights at Chelmno then established a small castle at Thorn (Torún), and gradually moved out

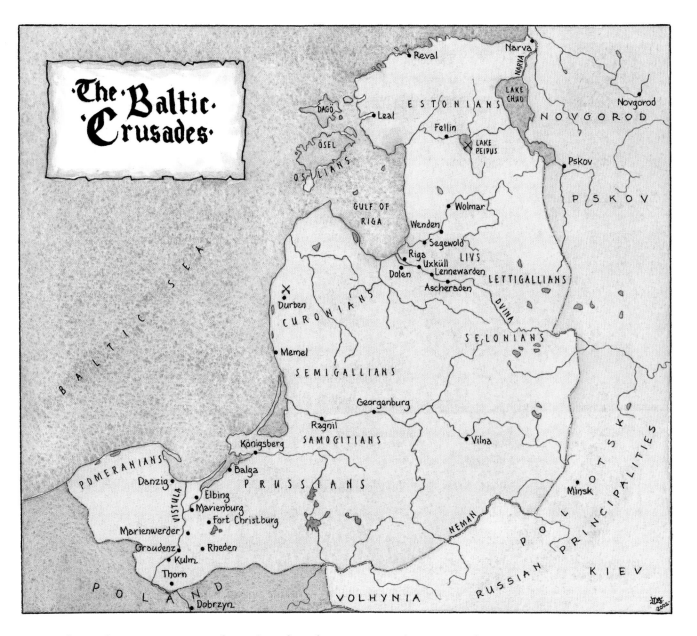

from there to a string of modest fortifications. By the 1240s they were pressing into the Orthodox territory of Pskov and Novgorod until they were halted, and dramatically defeated, on the ice of Lake Peipus on 5 April 1242 by Alexander Nevsky, Prince of Novgorod.

By venturing into Russian lands the Knights were responding to a papal desire to spread Latin Christianity in these regions. After the Battle of Lake Peipus this initiative was abandoned – the threat of the Mongol Golden Horde presenting, it was believed, a more immediate problem. For the most part, however, the Knights were in the regions along the Baltic for more mundane reasons: they could thus control the lucrative trade into Russia. But that was fraught with difficulties. In 1243 the Duke of Danzig decided that his own trade was being disrupted by the newcomers, and allied himself with the Prussians. Together they waged a decade of war against the Knights, which all but ended with the latter's defeat. Again in the 1260s the Knights were under pressure from their Prussian subjects. Their forts, which were still largely wooden, were overrun, their garrisons massacred, and the Knights were rescued only by a series of expeditions, in the form of crusades, led by members of the German nobility. Now the Knights rebuilt their vulnerable wooden forts in stone and, although there were further revolts by Prussian tribes, by the close of the thirteenth century they were no longer in serious danger of being dislodged from Prussia.

YEARS OF WAR

The Teutonic Knights in Prussia developed separately, and almost independently, of those in Livonia, where they took over from the Sword Brethren so disastrously defeated in 1236. Within 20 years they had recovered all the lands in Livonia that had been lost, and had even persuaded the King of Lithuania to become a Christian. It proved to be only a temporary arrangement. In 1259 the Teutonic Knights were defeated at Schoten. The Livonian Master then tried to make his way to Prussia, but he was ambushed at Durbe in 1260, and he and 150 of his knights were massacred.

The terrain he was trying to cross, between Prussia and Lithuania, was a wilderness, and one that could not support large armies. It was subject to massive snowfalls in the winter months, and massive flooding in the spring and early summer when the snow melted. Only in the depths of winter, when the snow was firm, or in the late summer when the floods had been dried up by the sun, was it really possible to wage war. Otherwise there were problems not just of supplying the troops but of the horses becoming bogged down in quagmires; it was just such a concern — that the horses might be lost in the swamps — that had contributed to the defeat of the Sword Brethren in 1236.

The battle at Durbe changed the minds of the Lithuanians. They abandoned Christianity and went to war with the Knights. The Estonians did likewise. War was joined for the next 40 years, a war in which the Knights were frequently defeated, and in which four of the Livonian Masters were killed. A Marshal of the Order was captured and burnt alive. By the end of the thirteenth century, however, some of the tribes had been pacified, and the remainder were watched over by the Knights from a string of castles.

Then, in the last years of the century, there was an attack on Livonia led by a Lithuanian Prince who was great-grandson to the King who had become a Christian. He formed an alliance against the Knights with the city of Riga, which had serious grievances against the Knights, so serious that they had taken them to Rome, defeated the Knights, killed their Livonian Master, and even made a modest incursion into Prussia. The Archbishop of Riga sided with the Prussian citizens, arguing that although the Teutonic Knights had entered the region to bring about the conversion of the pagans, their rapacious behavior had turned people away from the Church. The English Franciscan friar, Roger Bacon, whose life spanned most of the thirteenth century, had earlier made the same criticism, echoing Innocent III's earlier complaint about the Sword Brethren. He accused them of refusing to convert the heathen because they preferred to subjugate them.

Such charges were fairly frequent, but should not be taken at face value: Bacon, like other similar critics, had very little knowledge of the area in which the Teutonic Knights were operating. The Knights made a spirited defense of themselves, pointing out that although they were accused of trading with the heathen Lithuanians, they had a papal privilege to do so, and only traded in time of peace whereas the inhabitants of Riga themselves were doing it all the time. And as for being rapacious, they were only trying to reclaim what was rightfully theirs, won by the blood of some 200 brother knights, and countless retainers. Moreover, they added, in the lands for which they were responsible there were vast numbers of (Latin) Christians, and precious few anywhere else along the Baltic.

DIFFICULT TIMES

These were difficult times for the military Orders. In 1309, the year before the charges against them came to a head, the headquarters of the Knights was moved from Venice, where it was established after the castle of Montfort near Acre was abandoned, to Marienberg in Prussia. This had happened after pressure from the brother knights themselves. But despite this geographical shift the fact remained that they had been recruited, and the Order established, to defend the Holy Land. With the withdrawal from the Holy Land, even if it meant that the Teutonic Knights could concentrate all their forces on the northern frontier, the prime reason for their existence had disappeared. And, as will be seen later, the most powerful of all the military Orders, the Templars, like the Teutonic Knights, faced similar, though rather more lurid, accusations, arising from a king but backed, albeit reluctantly, by the Pope.

The Templars were destined not to survive. The Teutonic Knights did so. The

The Coronation of King Henry IV

move of the headquarters to Marienberg, within the Knights' own state, effectively put them out of the reach of secular rulers. And as for spiritual rulers, they diplomatically elected as Grand Master a Knight who could speak excellent French, at that time the language of the papal court.

Although crusades to the East had become impossible, the enthusiasm for crusading and its concomitant benefits, spiritual and temporal, had not. The Teutonic Knights in their northern fastnesses provided the opportunity. It became a practice, from 1304 onwards, that knights from across Europe, but especially from the German lands with which the Teutonic Knights had connections, would come to fight for a season, either in the winter or the summer *Reisen*, literally "journeys" but in practice mini-crusades. Among those who came were the King of Bohemia, Henry of Lancaster, and the future King Henry IV of England. The practice lasted a century, encouraged, perhaps, by the fact that European wars had trained many in fighting skills, as well as by the still-developing concept of chivalry. Perhaps as a sign that the notion of chivalry did indeed play a significant part, these journeys would begin with all the knights sitting down together and feasting, a "banquet of honor" as it was called. They then went to war under the banner of St George, the patron saint of knights.

The chief adversary of the Teutonic Knights was the Grand Prince of Lithuania, who was as ready to take the battle to the Knights as they were to him. So successful was Grand Prince Gediminas, to some extent diplomatically as well as militarily, that the Knights had to sue for a truce, then enter an alliance against him with the city of Novgorod, to the north of Livonia, which subscribed to Orthodox, rather than to Latin, Christianity. The Lithuanians responded by an alliance with Riga, to which the Knights were therefore obliged to lay siege, giving the Grand Prince free rein elsewhere.

A peace treaty was signed in 1338, but war broke out again after Gediminas' death, a war made all the more threatening because his son was now ruler of the Orthodox territory of Pskov to the East of Livonia. The Knights therefore found themselves surrounded. Crusaders were summoned from Prussia, but they failed to stem the advance of the Pskov-Lithuanian armies. In 1348 the Teutonic Knights had more success, aided not only by reinforcements from England and France, but by the outbreak of plague, the Black Death, which weakened both sides and diminished their ability to fight.

But rather as in the Holy Land, the Knights were too small in number, probably not amounting to more than 1,000 in total between Prussia and Livonia, to control the countryside. The Livonian Master built up a string of forts. He created a no-man's land between his territory and that of the Lithuanian Grand Prince. He re-established relations with Riga and succeeded in keeping the Poles from allying with the Lithuanians. He exploited divisions within their ruling house, and managed to ally himself with Jogailo, the grandson of Gediminas.

The alliance did not last. Jogailo did not trust the Livonian Master, and went to war again, using a new weapon against the Teutonic Knights – canon, which had been given to him as a present by the Knights only a few years before. The Knights responded similarly, but they were at a disadvantage: they had greater problems transporting their guns than had their adversary. Their situation became even more difficult when Jogailo married Queen Jadwiga of Poland. The Poles were also opponents of the Teutonic Knights, so there emerged a major force against the Order, though for the next half century or so the two countries, Poland and Lithuania, continued to be governed as separate nations. Potentially more threatening was Jogailo's decision in 1386 to become a Christian, thus undermining the claim of the Knights that in attacking him they were carrying out a crusade against the heathen. Though he promised to assist in the conversion of the Lithuanians, the Knights claimed that his baptism was only a political ploy. It was an argument that must have been widely believed, for it did not occasion a noticeable decline in the numbers coming from around Europe to take part in the summer or winter *Reise*.

ALLIANCES AND EXPANSION

The Knights continued to expand their lands, sometimes by purchase (Estonia had been bought from Denmark in 1346) as well as by war. Some of these acquisitions further hemmed in Jogailo – who, on his marriage, had changed his name to the more Polish-sounding Wladyslaw. A clash between the combined Lithuanian and Polish state and the Knights seemed inevitable, but the Livonian Master was of a different mind. He wanted a peaceful occupation of his territory, and persuaded Wladyslaw that both Knights and Poles had a common enemy in the emerging city of Muscovy. There was for a time an alliance between the two former enemies.

The alliance was dramatically ended partly through a change of Master but more immediately through a revolt in 1409 against the Knights by the Samogitians, one of the Lithuanian tribes they believed they had subdued. The new Master, unsympathetic to the policy of detente with the Poles pursued by his predecessor (who was, as it happened, his brother) seized territory which had been ceded to the Poles by the Knights in return for the alliance. Wladyslaw promptly allied himself with the rebellious Samogitians who were backed by their Grand Prince Witwold. The Lithuanians were, said Witwold, for the most part now Christians, and the Knights had no reason to oppress them. The war was no longer going to be against the heathen — it was to be between the Teutonic Knights and others, Poles and Lithuanians, who all professed the same faith. They were, indeed, rather better Christians, claimed Wladyslaw, than the Prussians who had by this time been governed by the Knights for nearly two centuries.

When the combined Lithuanian and Polish army marched on 1 July 1410, however, it was not against the Livonian knights but against those in Prussia. Prussia was still the headquarters of the Knights, and though the two branches by now acted fairly independently of each other, there was still a Grand Master with theoretical responsibility for both. However, when battle was joined on 15 July at Tannenberg only the Knights of Prussia faced the Poles and Lithuanians, strengthened by mercenaries from Central Europe, and even by Tartars. The odds were overwhelming, the defeat of the Knights catastrophic. More than 300 of them perished in the battle, the Grand Master was killed, and so too were most of the senior members of the Order.

The fortress at Marienburg did not fall, however. Its commander held out, waiting for the arrival of Knights from Livonia. They did not come, but even Wladyslaw, who was besieging Marienburg, thought that they might and that it would be advisable to withdraw: his army had also suffered considerable losses at Tannenberg, and his mercenaries were melting away. A treaty was agreed at Thorn in February 1411.

The Knights surrendered some territory to Poland, though not a great deal. More crippling was the vast sum they agreed to pay to Poland, so great a sum that it was the equivalent of ten years income for the King of England.

But that did not settle the matter. War broke out again in 1413 and yet again the following year. The Grand Master decided upon a more radical solution to his grievances against the Poles and Lithuanians. He appealed to a General Council of the Church.

THE COUNCIL OF CONSTANCE

The Council of Constance had been summoned in 1414 by a somewhat reluctant Pope John XXIII at the instigation of the Emperor Sigismund to end the scandal of a schism in the Church. The schism had begun in 1378 by the election of a rival claimant to the papacy, and had been further complicated by the choice of a third pope in 1409 at the Council of Pisa — which had itself been summoned in an attempt to end the schism. John was the representative of the Pisan "obedience", as it was called.

Apart from settling the schism — which it did — the Council was also required to adjudicate on a range of other issues, including the heresies of the Englishman John

Jan Huss at the Council of Constance

Wycliffe and the Czech Jan Huss — the latter it rather unwisely condemned to be burnt at the stake. The affair of the Teutonic Knights versus the King of Poland was pretty far down the agenda, but the debate which nonetheless took place was lively, and, in the person of Cardinal Pierre d'Ailly, Bishop of Cambrai and formerly Rector of the University of Paris, involved one of the most influential scholars of the day.

John Wycliffe

The spokesman for the Knights put their case to the Council early in 1415, before the Polish representatives had arrived. The argument was quite straightforward: the Teutonic Knights had been appointed to fight the heathen in Prussia and Lithuania, which they had done with considerable success: the Prussians were now Christians. The Polish King was envious of this success and had allied himself with the heathen in an effort to destroy the Knights. He had, moreover, failed to keep the terms of the treaty of Thorn.

Pope John XXIII, soon to be deposed by the Council, did not seem particularly impressed by the Knights' case. Even before it had been formally presented he denied that they had any rights to Lithuania, and appointed the Knight's enemies, Witwold and Wladyslaw, as his representatives for the Catholics in the Orthodox territories of Pskov and Novgorod.

The Polish case against the Teutonic Knights was put at the beginning of July by Peter Vladimiri, who was Rector of the University of Cracow. What he had to answer was the claim made on behalf of the Knights that they were proceeding legitimately because in their occupation of Prussia and Livonia they had been licensed to act by successive popes. Vladimiri's response was to say that the Pope had no authority to grant such rights, with the exception of the Holy Land. The Holy Land was an exception because this was Christian territory unlawfully seized by the Muslims; otherwise even heathen nations had a natural right to their own property. This was, indeed, the traditional view of theologians as held, for example, by Thomas

Aquinas. A century and a quarter later the same argument was to be used by the Spanish theologian Francisco de Vitoria, against the right of the Spaniards to wage war against the indigenous population of the New World. Vladimiri also pressed the point, again traditional and again repeated by Vitoria, that Christians could not coerce heathens, by force of arms, to become Christians. True conversion had to be freely made. Finally, recalling the provisions of the Truce of God, Vladimiri accused the Knights of breaking the prohibition of fighting on Sundays and feast days — though that was a prohibition, which, as has been seen, Thomas rejected.

THE END OF THE CASE

A defense of the Teutonic Knights was mounted by a German Dominican, John of Falkenberg. The arguments employed by Vladimiri were ultimately a condemnation of all crusades except those in defense of the Holy Land, or the reconquest of Spain. John defended crusades in principle on the grounds that attacks on the heathen were a means of protecting Christians. The Poles, he said, had used heathen troops to attack Christians, and that was an outrage. Wladyslaw's ambitions, he added, did not end with the conquest of Prussia but stretched as far as the Rhine. And he even, if obliquely, questioned papal authority in these matters. Imperial power in temporal matters, he argued, was older than papal, and had been given by God as a means to overcome his (God's) enemies, which is what the Teutonic Knights had been doing.

Pierre d'Ailly adopted a middle-of-the-road, conciliatory approach. Falling back on the feudal system and theories of chivalry he argued that everyone must fight for his lord, so there could be no complete ban on using heathens against Christians. Furthermore a pope, or an emperor, could order Christians to attack heathens to regain lost territory (as in the Holy Land), or to repress aggressive heathens, or to punish heathens who were attracting Christians away from their faith. The Bishop of Ciudad Rodrigo added that although it was true that conversion could not be brought about by coercion, armed force might nevertheless be used to bring about such conditions as would be conducive to missionary activity leading to conversion.

The theological arguments were finely balanced. Perhaps more persuasive with the Council fathers at the time were the *ad hominem* arguments produced by Wladyslaw and the Samogitians. The former claimed that he would have been off on crusade himself, fighting the Turks, had it not been for the need to deal with the Teutonic Knights in Prussia. And a delegation of Samogitians appeared before the Council to insist that they might already have been Christians were it not for the bad example of Christianity set by the Knights. The Knights rather went on to prove their adversary's point by arresting the Samogitians on their way home.

In the end the Council did not come down in favor of either the Polish King or the Teutonic Knights. But Witwold and Wladyslaw were left with their responsibility for the Latin Christians of Novgorod and Pskov, a sign that papal sympathies, at least, were on their side.

---

1. Quoted by Forey, Alan, *Military Orders and the Crusades* (Aldershot: Variorum, 1994) p. 211.

Chapter Six

Reconquista

*I*n July 1099, when in the Holy Land crusaders were in the full flush of victory after the capture of Jerusalem, on that other Christian-Muslim frontier, Spain, El Cid had just died. Born Rodrigo Díaz de Bivar about the year 1043, he belonged to the Castilian nobility – indeed, under King Sancho II he had for a time been commander of the armies of Castile. He fell out with Sancho's successor Alfonso VI, however, and was twice exiled. Though the epic poetry which recounts his undoubtedly extraordinary exploits tends to portray his prowess in battle as being directed against

El Cid

the Moors, operating mainly in the northeast of the Iberian peninsular, he was just as ready to sell his services to the Muslim rulers as he was to the Christian ones. In the last decade of his life, however, he had made common cause against the Muslims with the Christian kingdoms of Zaragossa and Aragón, establishing a power base at Valencia: he captured the city largely by subterfuge in December 1094. The Moors responded. In the battle of Cuarte which followed El Cid resoundingly defeated the Moors. It was the only major Christian victory against the armies of Islam in eleventh-century Spain. El Cid's achievements did not long survive him. In 1102 Alfonso VI relieved a siege of Valencia,

Alfonso I of Aragón — from a Neapolitan relief

now controlled by El Cid's widow, but made her burn down the city and retreat to Castile. El Cid's success nonetheless inspired the Christians of Spain: he never lost a battle, and that was true no matter on whose side he was fighting.

And the same, it was claimed, was true of Alfonso I, "the Battler", who in 1104 succeeded to the Kingdom of Aragón. Much of Alfonso's success, especially in the valley of the Ebro, was gained with the help of French knights who saw their involvement in Spain as an extension of the crusade — some indeed had already fought in the Holy Land. In 1118 Pope Gelasius II called a Council at Toulouse of French and Spanish bishops. He proclaimed a crusade against the Muslims of Spain, and an army was mustered and marched south. In December of that year it had captured Zaragossa. Next Alfonso marched westwards, to the border with Castile, then southward to Calatayud. And then south again. Invited by Christians living in the region of Granada, Alfonso's crusader-backed army arrived outside that city on 7 January 1126. He did not, however, attempt to lay siege to Granada. Instead he retreated to the mountains, where he was attacked by Abu Bakr, governor of Seville, whom he defeated near Lucena. Alfonso then pressed onwards to Malaga where he took a boat and sailed on the straits, an act of defiance to the Muslims who centuries

Notre Dame del Pilar on the Ebro River

before had crossed the same straits to attack the peninsular.

After that he marched back, taking with him many thousands of Christians from the south whom he then resettled in the Ebro valley. In the Muslim realms in Andalusia, however, there was consternation. Christian leaders there were forced into exile in Africa, so the net result in the south of the peninsular was, with the deportations and the emigrations, a population more solidly Muslim than it had been before Alfonso's dramatic invasion.

Once back in Aragón the series of Alfonso's victories continued. But it could not last. On 17 June 1134 his forces were finally overwhelmed, and three months later, on 8 September, he died. His extraordinary will has already been mentioned (cf. above, p. 83). He left to the Canons of the Holy Sepulchre in Jerusalem, to the Hospitallers and to the Knights Templar not the odd lordship or occasional ecclesiastical benefice but the whole of his Kingdom to be divided up among them. Why he did so can only be guessed at. It caused chaos: Alfonso's younger brother Ramiro had to be called back from his monastery to take charge. The Canons of the Holy Sepulchre were not then, and never became, a military Order able to prosecute the campaign against the Moors. And at that time it is unlikely, though not entirely out of the question, that the Hospitallers had yet developed their military wing. Only the Templars, a decade or so into their existence and with a rule recently granted, were in any position to fight on the Spanish frontier, and they were not particularly eager to do so, being already fully committed to the defense of the Holy Places. The one thing which may have attracted Alfonso to the Templars – and he had made his will three years before his death when still flushed with victory – was that if they could be persuaded to take up the Spanish crusade, then they would be prepared always to be present on the front line. The other forces the King could call upon, the local militias, were accustomed to serve only for a season of campaigning, and then return home.

RICH REWARDS

The Hospitallers and Templars were already known in Spain. The first grant made to the Hospital in the peninsular (in Catalonia) was as early as 1108, long before it was a military Order. The Templars, in which it seems some Spanish knights were already serving in the Holy Land, took part in the capture of Daroca, for which the Order in 1128 was rewarded with the lordship of Mallén in Aragón. Ownership of such estates did not of itself commit the Templars to fighting in the peninsular. They regarded these lordships as means of raising money, and possibly recruits, for the Holy Land, though in 1143 Templars were persuaded to fight in Spain, at first in the east and later elsewhere, and five years later Hospitallers were taking part in the siege of Tortosa, on the Ebro. Though neither the Temple nor the Hospital received all the estates that had been bequeathed to them in the will of Alfonso the Battler, nonetheless they were eventually awarded considerable holdings. In 1149, for instance, the Hospital received the castle of Amposta, and, at about the same time, the Temple received the castle of Calatrava, both of them frontier strongholds.

Calatrava was particularly important because it guarded the city of Toledo, the furthest significant outpost of the Kingdom of León. In the second quarter of the twelfth century Alfonso VII was King of León, a realm which consisted of León itself, of Castile to the east and Galicia to the west. South from Galicia was Portugal, ruled by Afonso, whom Alfonso rather thought of as a vassal.

Castle of Daroca

Afonso, however, did not see it that way. He thought of himself as an independent king, and acted independently. He was busy reconquering from the Almoravids the region between Coimbra and the Algarve, abetted in 1147 by an English fleet carrying crusaders to the Holy Land. The fleet paused its journey to assist in the capture of Lisbon with the consequence that the first bishop of the city was an Englishman.

Alfonso of León's victories over the Moors almost equalled those of his earlier namesake in Aragón, Alfonso the Battler. The King of León's success was aided by dissension among the Muslims, especially in the south of the country. The long-settled Moors in Andalusia resented the ruling Almoravids, part Islamic sect part dynasty, who were relatively recent arrivals from Morocco. By the mid-twelfth century Almoravid power was in any case crumbling, both in Spain and in North Africa, where it was being challenged by a new group, the Almohads.

The first part of the peninsular to break away from the Almoravid hegemony was the Algarve in 1144. In the southeast of the peninsular the Muslim Sayf al-Dawla was supported by Alfonso VII in his effort to set up in Murcia a kingdom independent of the Almoravids. When Sayf al-Dawla was killed, he was replaced by Muhammad ibn Sa'ad ibn Mardanish, whose name was shortened by the Christians to King Lobo.

Lobo was rather more Western-oriented than Eastern and was perfectly happy to recruit anyone who would help him overthrow the Almoravids. Other Muslims rulers also cooperated with Alfonso, including the ruler of Córdoba who made it possible for him, in 1147, to capture the Muslim fortress of Calatrava, which lay South of Toledo, guarding the road to Córdoba itself.

When the Almohads arrived in the peninsular from North Africa, the attitude of the Muslims of Andalusia changed. They had not wanted the Almoravids, but most of them (King Lobo was an exception) preferred to be ruled by the Almohads than by Christian overlords. Alfonso VII continued to lay siege to Muslim-held cities, but the Almohads had far more success against their co-religionists than had the Christian king: they took Málaga in 1154 and Granada the following year. Almería, which Alfonso had captured in 1147 with the assistance of fleets from

Above: Cross of the Knights of Calatrava

Italy and Barcelona (the port had been a base for pirates which the maritime powers wanted to disperse), was retaken by the Almohads in 1157, not long before Alfonso VII died. As the Almohads advanced, the fortress of Calatrava became increasingly vulnerable. The Templars who held it decided it would be too difficult to defend and, in any case, they claimed they were needed back in the Holy Land. In 1157 they handed over the fortress, given to them by Alfonso VII of León, to Sancho III of Castile, and departed.

THE CISTERCIAN CONNECTION

At this moment at the court of Sancho in Toledo there happened to be Abbot Raymond, of the Cistercian monastery of Fitero. He had come with a companion monk, Diego Velázquez, to confirm some gifts to his monastery. Diego was a former soldier with, the chronicles suggest, considerable experience of warfare. Diego urged his abbot to take over the fortress abandoned by the Templars, and this was eventually agreed. He did not, it seems, propose to defend it with monks, but with knights recruited from Fitero and from Toledo, whom he brought together in a new military Order, one taking its name, the Order of Calatrava, from the fortress they were setting out to defend.

There had been other, Spanish-based, knightly confraternities, inspired perhaps by the Muslim confraternities which guarded frontier posts, and to which men committed themselves in a quasi-monastic regime for a short period. Spanish historians are readier than historians of the Templars and Hospitallers to see an Islamic inspiration behind these confraternities burgeoning into religious Orders, possibly because in Spain Christians were more aware than they were in the Holy Land of Muslim traditions. But these confraternities, both the Christian and Islamic ones, were not religious Orders in the same way as were the Templars or the Hospitallers, because their members did not take permanent vows. Unlike the confraternities the Order of Calatrava was a true religious order. Like the Templars, it was inspired by the Cistercians, but, unlike the Templars, its members in practice actually became Cistercians: the knights it recruited were professed as Cistercian monks, and until his death in 1163 or 1164, both monks and knights were governed by Abbot Raymond.

On Raymond's demise monks and knights failed to agree on a successor, and a Master, Don García, was elected to take charge of the military wing. This did not break the link with the Cistercians. When in 1164 the new order was formally recognized by Pope Alexander III, so was its link with the Cistercians, and Fitero's mother-house, the abbey of Escaladieu, was given by the abbey of Citeaux itself the task of producing an appropriate rule. Eventually the abbey of Morimond became the monastery to which Calatrava was affiliated, and its rule was confirmed both by Pope Innocent III and by the general chapter of the Cistercians meeting at Citeaux in 1199. The rule of Calatrava was that of Citeaux, with necessary modifications to suit the military career of its members — the white habit of the Cistercians, for instance, was worn by the knights, but in a shorter length to enable them to mount their horses.

Like monks they were obliged to attend "office" in choir — recite the prayers prescribed seven times a day for monks and nuns — whenever they were either staying in a Cistercian abbey, or when they were at their headquarters. Whenever in such places the knights were on the same footing as monks, and their spiritual direction was entrusted to Cistercian monks. Only in two instances were changes made to the rule by the Master of Calatrava. Otherwise all such changes were made by the Abbot of Morimond or his representatives.

At about the same time as Calatrava was founded, in Portugal the Knights of Evora came into existence. The city of Evora had been conquered from the Moors in 1166: the Knights, a confraternity in the first instance, appeared the following year, following the rule of St Benedict. In 1187 it affiliated with the Knights of Calatrava, though maintaining a degree of (national) independence. They followed the rule of Calatrava, being dependent, like Calatrava itself, on the abbey of Morimond. In 1223, when the headquarters of the Knights moved definitively to Avis, it adopted the name of that city.

During the 1150s and 1160s the struggle against the Almohads, who were regularly reinforcing their troops from Africa via Gibraltar, was undertaken by the Calatravans, by the King of Portugal, Afonso, and by sundry adventurers, but also by King Lobo, who represented perhaps the major obstacle to Almohad expansion. But he was a Muslim, and his kingdom was often assaulted by Christians, including the

Templars from their castle of Daroca, despite the fact that he was a vassal of a Christian king, imported Christian settlers, and employed Christian troops. He died in March 1172. His dying instructions to his sons were to surrender his kingdom to the Almohads. He may have been worn out by the struggle against them, but more probably on his deathbed he decided to embrace once more the religion that he theoretically professed.

THE ORDER OF SANTIAGO

The anti-Muslim crusade in the Iberian peninsular was not helped by conflicts between the Christian kings. The realm of Afonso of Portugal was extended by an El Cid-like figure, one Geraldo the Fearless, but his success in capturing for Portugal Trujillo and Cáceres interfered with Ferdinand II of León's plans for the expansion of

Badajoz in Spain

his kingdom. In May 1169, for example, Geraldo was besieging Badajoz and asked Afonso for help. The garrison of the city appealed both to the Almohads and to Ferdinand. Ferdinand arrived and attacked Afonso – who suffered a broken leg while trying in vain to escape. Geraldo was forced to hand Badajoz to the Almohads, some other castles among his conquests to a Christian who was fighting as a mercenary for the Almohads, and Cáceres to Ferdinand. Ferdinand then made a treaty with the Almohad caliph, and founded the Order of Santiago to defend Cáceres.

That, at least, is one account of the origins of Spain's second, and somewhat unusual, military Order. It came into being on 1 August 1170 in Cáceres on the initiative of a Leonese, Pedro Fernández and a number of companions. How many companions is not certain, but it may have been thirteen, for "the council of the thirteen" became the ruling body of the Order. It seems at first to have been little more than a confraternity of local knights to defend their city. It took on the status of an Order together with the patronage of St James (Santiago) when, in 1171, the Master was admitted by the Archbishop of Santiago as a canon of his cathedral. It then undertook "to fight under the banner of St James for the honor of the Church and the propagation of the faith".

A religious Order, no matter how military, needed spiritual guidance. For Santiago this was provided by the Monastery of San Loyo, near Puente Minho, now Portomarín, where the original town, including its fortified church, has been rebuilt above the reservoir that has inundated the ancient stopping place on the pilgrim route to Santiago de Compostela. The monastery was one of Augustinian canons, and the canons provided chaplains to the knights of Santiago. It is possible that Pedro Fernández had originally wanted to have, like Calatrava, a Cistercian-based rule, but that approved by the papal legate Cardinal Jacinto in 1172, and by Pope Alexander III three years later, shows more Augustinian influence than it does Cistercian.

The Cistercians, perhaps, could not cope with the unusual feature that this order contained within its ranks not just clerics and laymen but married as well as unmarried laymen. Naturally for those who were married the rule had to be mitigated. They were not obliged to chastity but to marital fidelity. They were, however, required

Opposite: The great cathedral of Santiago de Compostela

to live celibate lives in the houses of the Order during the season of Lent and at other times in the course of the year, particularly the vigils of major feasts. The vow of poverty was also relaxed in their regard. When they were on campaign their wives and young children were taken into houses of the Order, as were their widows and daughters under the age of fifteen.

The Order of Santiago also took on the function of the Hospitallers, providing a hospice at León for pilgrims to the shrine of St James, and for lepers at Carrión, which was also on the pilgrim route. Soon after their foundation the Knights developed houses, and collected money, for the exchange and the ransoming of captives from the Moors, first at Cuenca and later at Toledo and elsewhere.

PROLIFERATION

By the 1170s the situation in southern Spain had radically changed, thanks to the arrival from Africa of the Almohad caliph himself. Under his inspiration the Moors began making inroads on Christian-held territory. Alcántara fell, and so did Cáceres despite the Knights of Santiago. But the caliph stayed only until 1176, and the Muslim advance faltered once more. Alfonso VIII of Castile set his sights on the Tagus valley, east of Toledo, and brought the military Orders into the area to subjugate and protect it — Templars, Hospitallers, Calatravans and the Knights of Santiago.

The military Orders in Spain now began to proliferate. Why this should have been so is not clear. It may be that, with the

A view of the Tagus valley

rivalry among the Christian kingdoms, each monarch wanted to have an Order that was, in some particular way, his own. If that was indeed the case, then they were to be disappointed. On occasion when a Christian king wanted to use the Orders in his realm against another Christian ruler, the Orders protested that their obligations bound them to fight Muslims, and they were therefore forbidden to wage war against fellow Christians. Or the number of different Orders may have reflected a wish on the part of the several monarchs not to allow any single one of them to become too powerful: Santiago, the Hospital and the Temple were already sufficiently aware of this attitude by 1178 to form a pact, later approved by the Pope, that they would unite to defend their rights, even against the King. Or it may just have been that the plethora of knightly confraternities turned themselves into full-blown military religious Orders more readily in Spain than elsewhere.

An example of this was the Order of San Julián de Pereiro, whose subsequent history also demonstrated the problems faced by the smaller Orders. It came into being at an indeterminate time, though it may have been in the early 1170s — it was confirmed by Pope Alexander III at the very end of 1177. At its head, in 1177 designated as "prior" which suggests at that time it was still a confraternity, was Don Gomez: by 1183 he was being called the "Master", indicating a change of status. The Order began on the border of Portugal and León (the spot, it is hardly a town, "Pereiro" is now in Portugal), and was favored by King Ferdinand II of León, who granted it the castle of Uclés, held hitherto by the Order of Santiago. Though it started as a separate institution, before the end of the 1180s it had affiliated itself to the Order of Calatrava, whose rule it followed — the sole exception being that its knights wore a green, rather than a red, cross on their white habits. The Knights of San Julián changed their name to the Order of Alcántara in 1217 when King Alfonso IX gave the castle of Alcántara to the Order of Calatrava, which in turn passed it on to the Order of San Julián. A further complication is that, when it came to be established in Castile towards the end of the twelfth century, it was known there as the Order of Trujillo.

A similar confusion of names occurred with another Order founded about this time, that of Montegaudio. Its founder was Rodrigo Alvarez, count of Sarriá, who had joined Santiago in 1167 but had left because the Order did not seem to him austere enough. In particular, it seems, he had problems with the admission of married men. Montegaudio's first castle was that of Alfambra in Aragón, given to it by Aragón's King Alfonso II. Alfonso was at odds with the Templars at the time, and rather wanted a local military order which he could himself control. Whether this was quite what Rodrigo himself had in mind is not so clear. He named his Order after the hill from which pilgrims to Jerusalem first saw the goal of their journey — Mount Joy — and he received some territory in the Holy Land, suggesting, perhaps, that he meant his Order to fight there. He certainly began, though did not complete, building a castle in Palestine. Meanwhile Rodrigo's desire for a stricter form of religious life appeared to be satisfied by affiliation directly with the monastery of Citeaux. This was approved both by the Cistercian General Chapter and by Pope Alexander III in 1180.

The link with the Cistercians did not last: Rodrigo proved to be a somewhat difficult character. By 1186, around the time of Rodrigo's death, there was talk of amalgamating Montegaudio with the Temple, probably because Montegaudio could not win enough recruits. King Alfonso was having none of it. Instead an amalgamation was arranged two years later with the King's own foundation of the Hospital of the Holy Redeemer at Teruel. This did not work out either, and in 1196 the possessions of the Holy Redeemer and Montegaudio fell after all to the Templars.

Not all members of Montegaudio or the Holy Redeemer were content to become Templars at the behest of the King. A dissident group set themselves up in the castle of Montfragüe in Castile as the Order of Montfragüe. They, in turn, sought union with the Order of Calatrava, which brought Calatrava into dispute with the Templars. Even the 1215 Council of the Lateran became involved, as did several popes, before the affair was eventually decided in favor of Calatrava in 1245.

DIFFERENCES RESOLVED

In 1201 Pedro II, King of Aragón, who was nicknamed "the Catholic", created the Order of St George of Alfama, named after its location near Tortosa on the Ebro — and after Pedro's devotion to St George. It was constituted by a number of Catalan nobles, and followed the rule of St Augustine as professed by the Knights Hospitallers.

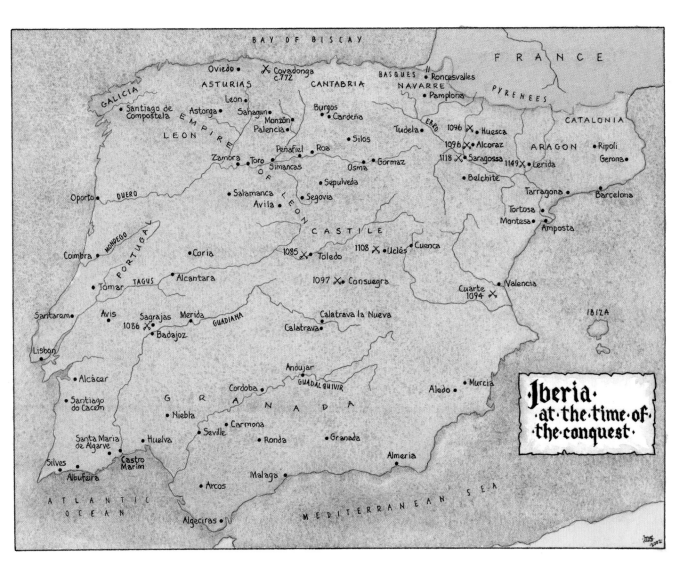

It had the odd fortune, however, not to be approved by the papacy for nearly two centuries. When this eventually happened, in May 1372, the bishop charged with ensuring that the Order was viable found it had only six knights, but ample funds.

All of this demonstrates one of the great weaknesses of the efforts made to recover Iberia for Christianity. In the mid-twelfth century the frontier between Muslim and Christians followed roughly the line of the River Tagus, though dipping south so that Calatrava was – just – inside Christian-controlled territory, then rising northwards to just south of Tortosa on the River Ebro. Unlike the Franks in the Holy Land, or the Teutonic Knights in Livonia and Poland, the Spaniards and Portuguese were fighting in what they considered their own territory. They had moreover a clear-cut objective: the recovery for Christianity of the peninsular from its Muslim invaders. But their efforts were hampered by the splintering of forces, and the rivalry between the Christian rulers of the several kingdoms – Navarre to the north, Aragón to the east, Castile in the middle, León to the west, and Portugal down the western seaboard.

In 1183 the Kings of Castile and León sank their differences in an agreement brokered by the bishops and the masters of the military Orders. They were to wage war against the Muslims, and not against each other. To meet this revived Christian threat the Almohads, recently preoccupied by rebellion in North Africa, came back in force to the peninsular. Alfonso VIII of Castile, however, did not long observe the truce with León, and seized some of the new King Alfonso IX's border castles. While Castile and León bickered, both kings thought it wise to make a truce with the Almohads. The energetic young Almohad caliph in 1190 and 1191 therefore advanced against Portugal instead, besieging en route castles held by the Order of Santiago, and one occupied by the Templars, which guarded the approach to Lisbon. They held out the first year; in the second two of the fortresses held by Santiago fell to the Muslims, and Portugal thought it advisable to make peace. The caliph returned to Africa, and there was a momentary lull.

It did not last. In 1191 Cardinal Jacinto, mentioned before as approving the rule of the Order of Santiago, became Pope Celestine III and renewed interest in Spanish crusade, especially because that in the Holy Land had recently suffered the enormous reverse of the Horns of Hattin (see above, p. 96). Celestine sent his nephew, Cardinal Gregorio, to broker a peace among the Christian kings. He was successful, and once again the Christians monarchs were on the march – or, at least, Alfonso VIII of Castile was.

Alfonso, supported by all the military Orders, marched out of Toledo to the castle of Alarcos, impatient for battle and not waiting for reinforcements promised both by Navarre and León. On 19 July 1195 he was confronted in the early morning by a Muslim force under the caliph. It was vastly superior in numbers, though the King did not at first realize it. In the battle that took place 25,000 Spanish knights were killed or made prisoner, including the Masters of Alcántara and Evora. The Master of Santiago was wounded, and nineteen of his knights killed. Though many of the

Knights of Calatrava also perished, their Master escaped unscathed. But they were too few in number successfully to garrison the fortress of Calatrava itself, which fell to the Muslims in the aftermath of the defeat at Alarcos, leaving Toledo dangerously exposed. A new headquarters was established at Salvatierra, even though it was within Muslim-held territory. In the September of 1213 this, too, fell to the Moors.

The disaster of Alarcos led to bitter conflict among the Christian kings. A determined crusade was needed, and Alfonso VIII decided to mount one. He got the support of Pope Innocent III who promised an excommunication on anyone who allied with the Muslims — which for a time included the other Christian kings in the peninsular. He got short shrift from Philip of France who was more worried about the English. He got the backing of the Archbishops of Bordeaux and Narbonne. The rallying point for the crusading force was Toledo.

Such French, mainly from the Midi, who were inspired by the thought of a crusade, arrived early in Toledo and, until they were stopped, massacred Jews to bide time. The King of Aragón was there, but those of León and Portugal, who were fighting each other, were not; some of their vassals turned up nonetheless. There were sundry bishops, sundry city militias, the Spanish Master of the Temple and the

Masters of Santiago and Calatrava. The army marched on 20 June. A week later it was before the fortress of Calatrava, which capitulated on 1 July. At which point most of the French, complaining of the heat, tore off their crusading crosses and went home, to the jeers of the Spaniards.

There were further Christian successes, but the departure of the French on the face of it weakened the crusading force and encouraged the caliph to the attack. The Christian army, however, was strengthened by the arrival of the King of Navarre. On 13 July 1212 the crusaders emerged from a canyon to find themselves face to face with a vast Muslim force, encamped on a

San Isidro

plain called Las Navas de Tolosa. The crusaders could not advance into the plain but a mysterious shepherd — whom the Christians later identified as San Isidro, the patron of Madrid, in disguise — told them of a secret path which brought them down beside their adversaries. There were minor skirmishes but battle was not joined until 17 July, which was a Sunday. The Christians all went to mass, and confessed their sins. When the lines were drawn up, the military orders were grouped in the center.

When the battle eventually began, the caliph against Alfonso VIII, it seemed for a time that the Christians were going to be defeated. It was only when the Christian rearguard was committed that the Muslims finally broke. But break they did. It was a Christian victory which far outdid the devastating defeat at Alarcos. News of the triumph was quickly broadcast around Europe.

Though no one could have known it at the time, it began the final chapter in the story of Muslim Spain. In the aftermath of Las Navas de Tolosa the Muslims fought back, but Alfonso VIII was determined to build on his success. Early in 1213 he captured the castle of Dueñas, which he handed over to the Order of Calatrava. The knights renamed it Calatrava la Nueva. He then took the fortress of Eznavexore, which the Order of Santiago, to whom he gave it, from then on called the Castellar de Santiago. The two military orders had the task, as the King moved on, of establishing Christian control over the countryside around their new strongholds, the work of more than a decade. Alfonso IX of León, who had not been at the battle, now, belatedly, joined in. He captured Alcántara, which he handed over to the Order of Calatrava: it had previously been held by the Hospitallers, but they were unwilling now to garrison frontier fortresses.

KINGDOMS UNITED

Alfonso VIII died in October 1214. His kingdom, and at the same period the kingdom of Aragón, were torn apart by civil war, and were in no position to further the reconquest. For a decade the prosecution of the war against the Almohads, and the defense of the gains made by Alfonso VIII, lay in the hands of the military Orders. The Orders collaborated against the Muslims in a manner which the Christian monarchs had too often failed to do. In 1217 the Orders were assisted in the capture of Alcácer do Sal by crusaders from the Rhineland and the Netherlands, stopping at Lisbon on their way to Egypt. When it was taken it was handed to the Order of Santiago, which had formerly held it, and the Order made it their Portuguese headquarters. In Spain the Orders of Calatrava and Santiago agreed to assist each other against the Muslims, despite any truce that the Christian kings might have agreed.

When the war was once again resumed, in 1224 under King Ferdinand III of Castile, it was the Almohad empire that was divided. Ferdinand allied himself with one side in the Muslim dynastic conflict, and with the aid of the Orders of Santiago and Calatrava successfully attacked the other. In any case the Almohad hegemony both in Andalusia and in North Africa was rapidly collapsing: by the end of the 1220s the Muslims in southern Spain could no longer look for assistance to North Africa. The last Almohad outposts beyond Andalusia were in the Balearic Islands. By the mid-1230s they too had been conquered by Jaume I of Aragón, and settled from Catalonia. The conquest opened up sea routes from Barcelona into the Mediterranean, which had hitherto been harassed by Muslim vessels sailing out of Majorca.

Jaume then pushed forward down the eastern seaboard towards Murcia. Valencia was weakened by internal dissent – one of its unseated Muslim rulers eventually became a Christian and handed his castles over to the Order of Santiago – and was finally starved into submission to Jaume in September 1238. In 1243 Murcia itself only escaped him by choosing to become instead a vassal of Castile, and it looked for a time as though there might be war between Aragón and Castile. This was only narrowly avoided by the Treaty of Almizra in March 1244.

By this time, however, a particularly significant event had occurred in the history of the peninsular. Alfonso IX of León died in September 1230. Ferdinand of Castile hurriedly laid claim to the throne of León, and it was conceded, thus uniting the two kingdoms – definitively as it turned out. This union of the two crowns enabled Ferdinand to concentrate his forces on the reconquest. By now, however, much of the fighting on the Muslim frontier was being undertaken by the Orders acting almost independently of the Christian rulers. They captured castle after castle – and then held on to them. They were particularly active in the southwest of the peninsular, in what is now the Algarve and Estremadura. They also assisted Ferdinand in the capture, in

June 1236, of the city of Córdoba, and left there a few knight to help garrison it.

SANTIAGO MATAMOROS

The military Orders were also heavily involved in Ferdinand's campaign to conquer Seville, which began in September 1246 and lasted until the capitulation of the city, cut off by land and its river blockaded, in November 1248. Part of the terms of the city's capitulation was the enforced exile of all its Muslim inhabitants. Some went to Jerez, still in Muslim hands, accompanied for their safety en route by the Master of Calatrava. Very many left the peninsular for North Africa. But most went to Granada, still a Muslim kingdom though one that was, after the Treaty of Jaén in January 1246, a vassal state of Castile. The ruler who entered this treaty, Muhammad ibn Yusuf ibn al-Ahmar, better known simply as al-ahmar ("the red"), built for himself the royal palace known as the Alhambra.

Edward I, King of England

Ferdinand of León and Castile died on 30 May 1252. Though there were many battles still to come, in his time the peninsular had effectively come under Christian rule: the surviving Muslim kingdoms had accepted him as its overlord. As well as his victories he had been the real founder of the University of Salamanca, and one of his daughters, Eleanor, the Infanta of Castile, married King Edward I of England. It was in one of the battles of Ferdinand's reign, at Jerez in 1231, after the Christians, as was their custom before launching their attack, had slaughtered all the Muslims captured earlier, that the Muslim army said they had seen St James, the patron saint of Spain, riding a white horse and bearing a white standard, leading the Christian army into battle; it was the origin of the image of "Santiago Matamoros", St James the Killer of Moors, that is so widespread in Spanish churches. Its iconography is almost indistinguishable from the crusaders' Saint George, except that a Muslim, rather than a dragon, lies beneath the horse's trampling hoofs. Ferdinand, who was buried not in knightly attire but the humble dress of a Franciscan, was declared a saint in 1671.

Ferdinand's successor, Alfonso X, faced a Muslim uprising across southern Spain in the middle of 1264. Fortresses fell once more to the armies of Islam; many Christians were slaughtered. Alfonso ordered the preaching of a crusade, and launched an attack on Granada, while Jaume of Aragón quelled Murcia. Alfonso then expelled most of the Muslims from Murcia, and brought in Christians from the north. Now only Granada remained, reduced once again to the status of a vassal kingdom. There was another revival of Muslim militancy, inspired by a new North African dynasty, the Marinids. They entered Spain in 1275 and won a number of victories against the Christians, including the battle of Moclín, near Granada, in 1280, when the Master of Santiago and nearly all of the knights of the Order were killed. Dynastic squabbles affected both the Marinid sultans and the Christian monarchs, but the Marinids kept a presence in the peninsular until 1340. On 30 October of that year Alfonso XI of Castile and Afonso IV of Portugal won a massive victory at Tarifa against seemingly overwhelming odds. Alfonso won so much gold and silver in booty that the price of precious metals fell on the Paris exchange. The Marinid sultan fled. None was ever again to invade the peninsular.

THE TEMPLARS SUPPRESSED

Yet Granada survived for another century and a half. The drive had gone out of the reconquest. Portugal had reached its natural borders, and looked to expanding into Africa rather than elsewhere in the peninsular. Aragón similarly turned towards the Mediterranean. The kingdom of León-Castile, which technically embraced a number of petty kingdoms, was not wholly stable, and in no condition to launch a major campaign. Succession to the crown of León-Castile frequently led to internal conflict into which the military Orders were dragged.

The remains of the fortress of Montessa

They, too, were now in decline. At the beginning of the fourteenth century the Temple was suppressed (cf. p. 173). It lands, declared the Pope, were to go to the Hospital, but this did not happen anywhere without problems, and particularly not in Iberia, where in any case the Pope said the Temple's holdings were to be reserved for him to distribute. In Aragón and in Portugal new military Orders were founded, respectively those of Montesa and of Christ. In neither kingdom was the monarch disposed to enrich further the already wealthy existing military Orders, probably for fear that they would become too powerful.

Montesa was founded in 1319 with ten knights from Calatrava under a Master, also from Calatrava, who took over the fortress of Montesa. The rule was that of Calatrava, though the title of the higher offices differed, and Montesa had non-professed knights in it as well as professed ones. As a strictly Aragonese Order it was placed under the spiritual jurisdiction not of the French abbey of Morimond, but that of Santas Creus, in Catalonia. The Order of St George of Alfama was incorporated into it in 1400.

In Portugal the Order of Christ took over all the property of the Templars, including their headquarters at Tomar, though the Knights of Christ were first established at Castro Marim on the River Guadiana, which marks the Spanish-Portuguese frontier. They, too, took the rule of Calatrava, and their spiritual direction from the Cistercians — in this case from the abbey of Alcobaça. Its first Master came from the Order of Avis. The immense wealth of the Order of Christ was used to fund Portuguese expansion overseas.

The problem for all the Orders was that they effectively constituted the main, if not the only, standing army of the country in which they were situated. Whereas in their early years they had frequently operated independently of the monarchs, as time went on they became increasingly subject to their interference. Once the Orders began to insist, Santiago from 1259 and Calatrava from a slightly later date, that their knights were drawn only from the ranks of the nobility, it was inevitable that they would be dragged into the internal politics of Castile and the other kingdoms. Even before that, the kings of Castile had demanded a say in the elections of the Grand Masters. In 1326, when the Master of Calatrava was deposed for alleged cowardice in the face of the enemy, the Abbot of Morimond reinstated him, as was his right, only to find that a royal nominee had been appointed in the interim. In 1342 the King of Castile appointed his own son, seven years old and a bastard, as Master of Santiago. In protest the Master of Calatrava locked himself in his castle. He was besieged by the King's men, and beheaded when the castle was forced to surrender. The Orders were simply too wealthy, and therefore too powerful, to be allowed to go their own way.

Not that the numbers of knights were very large. Although they were given numerous castles, few of them were garrisoned wholly, or even at all, by professed knights. Many were held by vassals of the various Orders, which meant that their wealth could be used when necessary to hire mercenaries. Though kings often asked for a specific number of Templars or Hospitallers or others to serve on the frontier or in particular campaigns (in 1303 Jaume II of Aragón wanted 100 Templars, 60 Hospitallers, 30 of Calatrava and 20 of Santiago) it is not clear that the orders provided the men – or whether they served themselves or brought in vassals or mercenaries. When, in 1280, thanks to the imprudence of the Grand Master, Santiago was nearly wiped out at the battle of Moclín, the total of knights killed, in addition to their Master, was only 55. Yet too few remained for the Order to be viable. Alfonso X decided to reinforce it by amalgamating Santiago with the Order of Santa María de España, which he had himself founded only in 1272 on the model of Calatrava – and subject spiritually to the French Cistercian abbey of Granselve – to control the Straits of Gibraltar. Santa María was founded as exclusively a maritime Order, the only one of its kind, but in 1281 it was incorporated into Santiago, thereby losing its name and its specific purpose.

Isabella of Castile

GRANADA

With the Christian kingdoms torn by internal squabbles and sometimes open warfare with their Christian neighbors into which the military Orders were inevitably drawn whether they wished it or not, there was little time or appetite for crusading in the later fourteenth, and the first 75 years or so of the fifteenth, century. But in 1474 Isabella became Queen of Castile and five years later her husband Ferdinand succeeded to the throne of Aragón. "Los reyes católicos", the Catholic monarchs, finally turned their attention to completing the reconquest, abetted by a dynastic struggle within Granada. The campaign was hard fought, as Ferdinand laid siege to, and captured one by one, the towns of the Kingdom of Granada. At the battle of Loja in 1482 the Masters both of Santiago and Calatrava were killed. Six years later the Master of Montesa died at the battle of Beza. The siege of Granada itself began in April 1490. There were, it was reported, 10,000 knights. Of those, the Order of Santiago had fielded nearly 1,000, with some 2,000 foot soldiers. The number of knights provided by the Order of Calatrava is not recorded, but it was probably some 400. Alcántara produced 266, the Hospital 62.

Granada fell on 2 January 1492. It was Diego García de Castilo, Acting Grand Master of the Order of Calatrava, who that morning raised the Christian standard over the Alhambra. Like the rule of *los reyes católicos*, the Inquisition, which Ferdinand and Isabella had created in 1478, was now imposed over the whole of Spain. Jews and Muslims alike were offered baptism. The alternative was exile. The reconquista was over.

Chapter Seven

Rule of Life

The strange idea of monks who were also warriors was a new one, but criticism of this new form of religious Order in the Church was fairly muted. Perhaps it was Bernard of Clairvaux's endorsement of the Templars in *de laude novae militiae* that gave the Templars respectability. Yet it had taken three requests from the Templar's founder, Hugh de Payen, before he had produced this panegyric. It may be that he, too, originally had doubts about combining the roles of monk and knight, but if so he overcame them. It was certainly acceptable to fight the devil's challenges to the soul, he argued, and it was equally acceptable to fight the enemies of Christianity. It could not but be right, therefore, if one Order encompassed in its members both kinds of combat.

It was a seductive argument, and appears to have persuaded most of his contemporaries, some of whom borrowed from his little treatise to write their own praises of the Templar life. Not that critics were entirely lacking. The great abbot of Cluny, for example, Peter the Venerable, who had sponsored the translation into Latin of the Qu'ran, wrote to the Pope denying that the Templars constituted a religious Order at all. They were, he seemed to suppose, just another confraternity of knights. Issac of Stella, the English-born abbot of the French Cistercian monastery of Étoile ("Stella" – star), was outright condemnatory. The Templars, he said, constituted a new "monster", its members recruited to force Muslims into Christianity (a charge which certainly was not true) and to kill those who would not conform (which, on the whole, did not prove to be true either).

Thomas Aquinas

There were many criticisms of the way of life of the various Orders of knights in the course of their history, but the notion that they did not constitute an "Order" in the proper religious sense soon ceased to be one of them. When, in his *Summa Theologiae*, Thomas Aquinas discussed the religious life, he raised the question whether a religious institute can be founded for military service.[1] In the manner of the schoolmen Thomas first puts the objections. He quotes the Gospel of Matthew about turning the other cheek, but this refusal to counter evil, he says, is contrary to the duty of a soldier, and he then adds three extra objections, which rather turn on the niceties of medieval canon law. As for tolerating evil, says Thomas in response to Matthew, it depends against whom the evil had been committed. If it were against oneself, then it is right to turn the other cheek, but it is wrong to tolerate the evils done to others. It is even a sin, he says, if one can "readily restrain the wrong doer". And that, he believes, is the role of the military religious Order.

The argument is fairly cursory, but by the time Thomas was writing his *Summa* even the Spanish military Orders had existed for a century with the Church's approval, and the Templars for a good while longer. The Templars had a rule, approved by the Council of Troyes, which was both a spiritual document, laying down their religious obligations, and a practical one, detailing matters of clothing and behaviour. Some of the instructions seemed precisely aimed at limiting the excesses of knightly pride, and of knightly behavior. They were to be humble men with limited resources (the seal of the Templars shows two knights bestride the one horse, though knights were allowed three mounts). There was to be no jousting and they were not to go hunting – though an exception was made for hunting lions "which come searching for what they may devour". In the case of the Teutonic Knights an exception was made for hunting wolves and bears – though they must not do so with dogs.

The military Orders were all very similar. When the Teutonic Knights were founded with a dual purpose of fighting and caring for the poor and sick, they simply took the rule of the Templars for the fighting men, and the rule of the Hospitallers for those who cared for the sick. All who joined a military Order were bound by the same three vows, taken by anyone who entered a monastery or convent – poverty, chastity and obedience – though the Order of Santiago was necessarily different as far as chastity went because it recruited married men.

Recruits to the monastic life were required to go through a period of probation in the novitiate. This does not seem to have been as true in the military Orders. Indeed, in the Hospitallers and the Order of Santiago there does not seem to have been any provision at all for a time of spiritual training and instruction in the rule and way of life of the Order. Those Orders which were linked to the Cistercians – Calatrava and Avis – had a year-long

Grey Abbey, a Cistercian Abbey in County Down, founded in 1113

probationary period like the monks, and the Templars and those who copied them did likewise, but it seems that it was only occasionally enforced except in the Teutonic Knights which retained the noviceship.

It has been suggested that entrants to the military Orders had less to learn than those who became monks. Certainly, as has been seen, one of the attractions of Templars and others was that its recruits were not for the most part embracing a life wholly alien to that which they had lived before entry. They were still knights and, as knights, their fundamental skills in fighting with the sword or lance would have been learnt from childhood, charging with practice lances against a target, which was often built in the shape of a Saracen.

It is unlikely that the majority of them were literate, again an important distinction from men who become choir monks, obliged to sing the office, which changed from day to day and liturgical season to liturgical season. Indeed, the rule of the Templars presupposes that they would not be able to read the office books. They were to attend office in choir whenever the Order's priests were present in sufficient numbers to sing it, but otherwise instead of the psalms and readings which made up  the office, and which changed according to the time of the year, they said Pater Nosters and Ave Marias, repeating them seven times a day according to the traditional canonical hours. It was not even expected that all new recruits would know these simple prayers. They had to learn them – together with the creed – within six months of joining, said the Teutonic Knights, and the Teutonic Knights were, at least for a time, punctilious in testing whether recruits had acquired the knowledge. New members of the Templars who did not even know when to stand, kneel or sit during the divine offices were advised to take seats at the back of the chapel, so they could watch what the others did.

Cross of the Knights of the Teutonic Order

Knowledge of the rule was important. Various of the Orders laid down that the rule, or a section of it, should be read aloud to members every Sunday, or every month, or every two months. But it was necessary that at least one person in every house knew in detail what the rule said, for instance about admissions to the Order, so it must have been taught fairly well even though very few copies of these rules seem to have survived. That may mean that few were made. It might also mean that a good many simply fell apart through heavy use.

Admission was, usually, a local affair. Very few would-be Templars or others traveled to their chosen Order's headquarters to ask to be allowed to join. Most entered the house of the Order nearest to where they lived, which would have meant that they were well known to the knight in charge of the local commandery (or preceptory). Only the Templars and the Hospitallers recruited widely across Europe – the others drew their membership largely from Germany, in the case of the Teutonic Knights, or Spain and Portugal for the Iberian ones. Even so, a Hospitaller recruited in England or one recruited in Spain was very unlikely to move far from home, apart perhaps from a couple of years at the front, or in headquarters. They were therefore, in their commanderies, able to act as local administrators of justice, or even play significant roles in the national life of their country though, perhaps curiously, very few of the clerical members rose to important posts in the Church hierarchy. Permission to join could not be taken for granted; the commander was expected to consult his council, and abide by a majority decision. Candidates were expected to be healthy, unmarried (except, of course, for the Order of Santiago) and not betrothed to anyone. They could not be serfs, or in debt. The average age of entry was eighteen or more years old, and according to a slightly later provision, entrants were supposed to have been knighted before they joined. Very many who joined traditional monastic houses had entered them as child "oblates", placed in the monastery by their parents when they were still quite young. This was not the case for the military Orders, even though they sometimes found themselves for one reason or another looking after children. Again, Santiago was the exception, as it had to provide for the children as well as the wives (or widows) of its married members.

Knight of the Teutonic Order

Why men chose the life of a member of a military Order is not easy to determine. The earliest knights no doubt acted out of a zeal for saving their souls, and serving the Church, in the way they knew best. As time went by motives changed. Very few recruits were of the highest nobility. Though Grand Masters might sit in the Cortes of the Spanish Kingdoms, or be accepted as princes of the Empire, chances of high office were slim. But local administrative duties were common, and appealed to the middle-ranking nobility; it is from that class, for example, and from the administrative class of the Empire, that recruits came for the Teutonic Knights.

The expense of knighting the recruits, if this had not already been done, had to be borne by the families they were leaving behind, who also might be expected to give a substantial donation to the Order to gain admission for their son. The matter of a donation was, however, rather problematic. It sounded too much like simony, the crime of exchanging holy things for money. Pope Innocent III tried to forbid the practice, and the Fourth Lateran Council, which he called for November 1215, condemned it. But it did not go away. The Order of Santiago continued to demand a "dowery", at least for non-knights who were entering. The Teutonic Knights did not demand that anyone who had committed simony should be expelled, though the Templars were stricter.

Those joining, of course, were not all knights, actual or potential. The Orders all needed clergy, and these were difficult to recruit because for clerics so many different career paths were open once they had been ordained – and the clergy were always recruited as already ordained priests. There were also sergeants, fighting men who were not knights, and there were servants as well as, in some instances, slaves. Some of the servants were members of the Orders, like Cistercian lay brothers: the Teutonic Knights rather picturesquely called them "half brothers". These servants were important to the Orders, providing much-needed skills such as that of blacksmith, or agricultural skills in the commanderies.

Then there were others, as likewise in monastic communities, who associated themselves with the Orders through their donations, and who in return for the support might expect to be buried by the Order, and whose souls would be prayed for by the brethren.

There were also, it should be added for completeness' sake, some nuns who were members of the Orders. "Women's company is a dangerous thing," said the Templar rule, "for by it the ancient enemy [the devil] has led many away from the straight path to Paradise." But not all the Knighthoods were so forbidding. It is clear enough how houses for women following the rule of the Order of Santiago came to be established: the Order had to make provision for the wives and daughters of members, and the convent of Sigena in Spain survived with a community of nuns in the distinctive habit of the Order down to the Spanish Civil War. More puzzling is the origin of the communities of nuns belonging to the Hospitallers. It seems highly unlikely that they arose because women played a part in caring for the sick and the poor in the hospitals of the Order. It is more probable that individual women associated themselves with particular houses, and imitated the life of the brethren as best they could. Towards the

Above: The Round Church, Little Maplestead in Essex, built by the Knights Hospitallers in 1190

end of the twelfth century they were gathered together in convents, some of which housed fairly large numbers — that of Buckland in England, for example, had a community of around 50 right up to its suppression at the Reformation. The Teutonic Knights, on the other hand, did have women working in their hospitals, and treated them as members of their Order: they were called "half-sisters".

Convents of nuns depended for support and spiritual guidance on the religious Order with which they were associated. Although there was a degree of internal democracy — rather greater, perhaps, than in the male equivalent — they were ultimately responsible to, and the responsibility of, the prior of the particular Knighthood in that region. One of his tasks was to provide a chaplain from within the Order. Like the male commanderies they paid their responsions, that part of their income, a third, which went to support the crusades. The life of these nuns, though enclosed behind convent walls, was on the whole not as demanding as that in other religious Orders for women — which may have been their attraction for families wishing, for whatever reason, to place their daughters in a nunnery. Compared to membership of the Knights, however, the number of nuns associated with the military religious Orders remained quite small.

Because recruits to the military Orders were frequently admitted without a period in a novitiate, so that a knight or a sergeant taking his vows (was "professed") commonly followed immediately upon his admission to the Order, some means had to be found to make clear to the new member what it was they were undertaking. In the course of the ceremony of profession a recruit was therefore constantly reminded of the obligations he was taking on, the commitment to the three vows of poverty, chastity and obedience, and the hardships of the life he was embracing. He was given an opportunity to withdraw and, as this was quite probably the only time a recruit had ever heard anything of the details of the rule, it would be surprising if some had not done so.

They entered the Order in different ranks — knights, sergeants or servants. Distinctions in status did not at first matter greatly — they became more pronounced as time went on — though those entering as knights had to be from knightly families. All were called "brother", whatever rank they enjoyed. The early egalitarianism did not last. In the early thirteenth century Hospitaller knights were give precedence even over the priests of their Order. There were other distinctions. Knights, for example, were provided with three horses, sergeants only with one, though as sergeants did not take part in cavalry charges one was all that was necessary. The sergeants were foot soldiers, though they might ride horses, just as knights who constituted the heavy cavalry might very often find themselves fighting on foot. Membership of the knightly class was more restrictive than that of the sergeants. Not only had the former to be from knightly families, they were supposed to be of legitimate birth, though this might be waived. They also had to be free of debt, and uncommitted in marriage, not even betrothed. Married men could of course always enter Orders, military or otherwise, if their spouses agreed, and likewise agreed to become nuns. On becoming nuns they did not have to join a convent associated with the Order of which their husband was a member.

ROLES

As the centuries passed it became increasingly difficult to gain admission to these Orders. Even by the end of thirteenth century the Hospitallers were discouraging the recruitment of knights, though that may very well have been because of financial considerations – the cost of maintaining a knight with his armor and three horses (not to mention his servant) was enormous. Later still, as the need for fighting men declined and the Orders became increasingly status-conscious, admission was restricted to those who could demonstrate that their parents on both sides had been of noble birth.

The vocation to a military Order had always been an odd one, but after the fall of the Holy Land to the Muslims, the fall of Granada to the Christians and the pacification and conversion of Livonia and Prussia, it became odder still. The proportion of men joining the Orders who were sent out to do battle with Muslim or pagan was always fairly small, at least at any given moment. The majority were engaged in recruiting drives, and looking after the sources of revenue which financed the expeditions. They might expect to serve at the "front" for a period, whether in Spain or the Holy Land, but very few would have stayed there all their lives. They might also expect to spend some time in the central headquarters of their Order, another posting which might draw them away from their home country, but again this was for most a temporary appointment.

At home, however, they moved between commandery (or preceptory, the two terms were indistinguishable) and commandery, though rarely out of their province (or "priory") into which the commanderies were organized. The commandery was the basic unit. It might be a small community of knights (or even a single knight), sergeants and serving brothers, or a large one with several knights. The purpose of the commandery was to raise funds from its lands, a third of which (the "responsion") was to be sent every year to headquarters for the support of the knights on crusade. Thanks to donations, the military Orders became possibly the largest property owners in a given territory — certainly the Hospitallers seem to have become the largest landowners both in England and in the Kingdom of Aragon. The commanderies meant that the locally based knights had all the tasks of landowners. They needed skilled artisans — ploughmen, blacksmiths and so on — to look after their farms. Some of these were members of the Order; most would have been employed for the purpose. With land holding went certain duties in a locality, the administration of justice, for example, with which the life of the knight on the commandery would be bound up. In other words the knight in his commandery led the style of life of a medieval country gentlemen.

Emphasis on the material advantages of life in the commanderies of these orders, and especially when the brothers were away from the frontline against the Muslims, should not be taken to mean that many of the recruits had not joined for spiritual reasons. They joined, they said, to save their souls, an understandable preoccupation for men whose career was fighting. Though Humbert of Romans, the Master-General of the Dominicans between 1254 and 1264, complained of the military Orders squabbling among themselves, he nevertheless praised the Teutonic Knights for their piety towards the Virgin Mary, and for their observance of the vow of poverty.

If there was a large group living in the commandery, and a chaplain, then conventual life — that is, the regulated, orderly life of a monk might be attempted, as it was in the castles of the Holy Land. This is what the rule laid down, the requirement, incumbent on all members of religious Orders, to attend "office" seven times a day, from Matins at four in the morning to Compline last thing at night, after which the "great silence" would have been observed until the following day. In the early years knights and sergeants lived in dormitories, and all fasted on a good many days of the year, as well as abstaining from eating meat for almost half of every week, and all the way through Lent and Advent. Despite this, the regime was not as harsh as in the monasteries. These after all were fighting men, who had to maintain their health and strength for the battlefield.

Even on a campaign the practice of their faith was central to their life. The tents of the knights were placed in a circle around the tent that served as a chapel – and the chapel tent was the rallying point in case of a surprise attack. In 1344 the Teutonic Knights got permission when in the field to start Mass before dawn, and office was said as far as possible at the regular canonical hours at a field altar, within the hearing of those guarding the camp.

Some may have had a genuine calling to this way of life. It was suited to a member of the knightly class, and a devout knight might very well have been attracted to the idea of committing himself to a religious vocation by taking the traditional vows of poverty, chastity and obedience. These Orders were, after all, founded at a time when there was an interest in, and a renewal of, religious life in the Church. Indeed, the military Orders could claim to be the first true religious congregations. The form of monastic life was quite different: monks entered a particular monastery and stayed there, at least in theory,

Castle of the Knights of St John, Rhodes

for the rest of their lives. The monasteries were self-governing, and independent of each other. This had begun to change, first with the Cluniacs and then with the Cistercians, but the centrally governed and regulated Templars and Hospitallers were a more radical departure from the norm, and one that the Orders of friars, Dominicans and Franciscans, were to imitate at the beginning of the thirteenth century. There was, moreover, much less of an emphasis on literacy in the military Orders than in the traditional ones, so someone who felt himself called to a form of religious life but was not able to read or write might prefer to choose one of or other of the military orders.

For any devout person entering a religious order to secure his or her salvation it was important to believe that the life he was embracing, one according to the rule of the Order he was joining, was a sure route to paradise. And one way of demonstrating that that was so was to produce saints: to have the founder declared a saint was especially important. It is, then, rather odd that, with the exception of the Knights Hospitallers, none of the military Orders boasted that they had fostered saints among their ranks. The Templars did indeed lay claim to one saint, but, though a crusader he turns out not to have been a Templar himself. The Hospitallers laid claim to four saints from these foundation years: there was a cult of the first two Masters, and two members who died in the early thirteenth century were formally canonized. In the lives of neither of the two canonized saints, however, was military prowess a significant feature. Both of them came from what is now Italy.

Life within a military Order might lead to sanctity, but it was not without its worldly compensations. When a recruit was admitted he handed over all his clothing, and received new armor, clothes, even underwear, from the Draper (as the quartermaster was entitled). This was a sign to demonstrate that the recruit had taken the vow of poverty, and, once the vow had been pronounced, a member could not own anything of his own. He could not even make a will because that would imply he had personal possessions to dispose of as he wished. Anyone who at his death was found to have private property could be refused a Christian burial. Nonetheless, a Hospitaller, or a member of the Order of Santiago, might expect to live a fairly comfortable existence with, unless he was personally so inclined, few of the ascetic practices which marked the stricter Orders in the Church – and it was accepted that a particularly devout knight might leave his Order for one that was more strict.

Chastity was more problematic. There were no more or less strict interpretations of this vow, it was an absolute prohibition of sexual activity of any sort, but failure to observe it was not treated as seriously as some other crimes. For the Templars, sexual intercourse with a woman was counted a less heinous offence than an act of simony, of killing a Christian, or even of leaving a castle by other than the prescribed exit. Sodomy was, however, counted among the most serious failings, which justified expulsion from the order – a provision added rather late to the rule, which suggests that early on it had not been a problem. Intercourse with a woman was on the same level as loss of Templar property: both entailed no more than a year's loss of the habit – though such misdemeanors would have damaged a knight's career in the Order. Not all members were as observant of the vow of chastity as they might have been, especially as the first enthusiasm passed into history. In 1451, for example, the Master of the Order of Alcántara sought, and received, authorization from the Pope to leave his fortune to be divided among his fourteen illegitimate children.

Rules were enforced through weekly "chapters" – at least in those houses that had sufficient numbers to maintain some kind of conventual life. The chapters were gatherings of all professed members in a commandery, during which not only were the problems of the commandery discussed, but individuals were punished for infringements of the rule. This was on the local level; there were also chapters at the level of the "priory", and similarly at the headquarters of the Order. There would also be an annual "general chapter", attended by representatives from the priories or provinces – the general chapter appointed the Templars' provincial masters or the Hospitallers' priors, and the provincial masters and priors were responsible to the general chapter. It was the role of the general chapter to make such adaptations of the rules as were necessary, to oversee the financial interests of the Order, and, at the death or retirement of a Grand Master, to elect his successor.

The Grand Master was the chief executive officer of the Order, responsible for its overall spiritual and financial health. His powers were limited both by the rule, which of course applied to him as much as to anyone else, and by the requirement that he consult his council about major decisions – which included making a truce with the

Muslims. Though some Orders, such as Thomas of Acre or the smaller Spanish ones, had too few members to merit a range of officers, in the larger ones the Master was assisted by a number of officials. In the Templars, for instance, these included the Seneschal, who was the Grand Master's deputy and the Order's standard bearer, the Marshal, in charge of all military affairs, the Draper already mentioned and the Turcopolier, who had charge of all hired troops. There were other officers close to the center of affairs: the Commander of the Kingdom of Jerusalem, for example, was the Order's treasurer — a particularly significant task as the Templars developed their banking system (cf. below).

General chapters were made up of local commanders serving in the East, and masters of the major divisions — provinces in the case of the Templars, "langues" or "tongues" in the case of the Hospitallers. As was remarked earlier, the other military Orders were almost entirely regionally based though the Teutonic Knights had commanderies elsewhere as well as Germany, including some in Spain, while in 1250 the Order of Santiago undertook a recruiting drive in Germany. The two sets of divisions, into provinces or "langues" based on the strength of the presence of the Templars and Hospitallers in the different parts of Europe, were very similar: Apulia, Aragon, England, France, Hungary, Poitou, and Portugal for the Templars, Aragon, the Auvergne, Castile, England, France, Germany and Italy for the Hospitallers. In the Hospitallers certain senior offices became associated with the head of the different "langues", and eventually members of a "langue" at the Order's headquarters on Rhodes came to have their own "auberge" or hostel. This style of government by chapter, with a few minor differences both of terminology and of practice, was common to all the military Orders, for they all to some extent modeled themselves on the Templars, the first one to establish a rule. (The Cistercians, with whom of course several of the Orders were linked, had a somewhat similar structure.)

The chain of commanderies around Europe, together with the fact that knights regularly traveled between the commanderies and to their headquarters, enabled the Templars to develop a banking system both for

Henry III

themselves and for others. It is unclear how the bank began, perhaps by the Templars's castles serving as depositories for the valuables – documents, money, jewels – of those going on crusade. But use of this facility was not restricted to crusaders. The English King Henry III put his crown jewels first in the London Temple, and then in that of Paris, the latter a huge fortress just outside the city which eventually became the center of the Templars' financial dealings. King Henry went on to use the jewels as security against a loan to raise money to fight Simon de Montfort.

Königsberg, headquarters of the Teutonic Knights

In the early years the Templars mainly restricted their banking operations to supporting the crusades, but in the thirteenth century banking became a serious undertaking in its own right, and many of the Order's clients had little or nothing to do with the crusades. There was in Paris a cashier on duty several days each week, repaying money deposited, or receiving new funds: even the papacy channeled money through the Paris Temple. In the Middle Ages banking was a problematic way of producing income. Usury, the lending of money for interest, was then strictly forbidden as being against Christian teaching. There were, however, a number of ways round this prohibition, and the Templars, who kept meticulous records, possibly made gains from the "spread" of exchange rates when converting currency, and perhaps through charging for banking services rendered.

Occasionally the deposits people had made were raided – as, for example, when the Templars were called upon to raise money for King Louis's ransom (cf. above, p. 108). The Templars themselves, however, had a reputation for probity, as was demonstrated on that same occasion. But they also had a reputation for being a very wealthy Order in the Church. At the beginning of the fourteenth century this reputation was to be their undoing.

---

1. *Summa Theologiae* IIa IIae, quaestio 188, articulum 3.

Chapter Eight

A ftermath

*T*he Templars' castle at Acre, the last Christian fortress in the Holy Land, fell on 14 August 1291. The crusaders, together with many of the Franks who had made their home in the Latin Kingdom of Jerusalem, fled to Cyprus.

Cyprus was itself a Christian kingdom, ever since it had been captured in 1191, as he was passing, by the English King Richard I, Richard the Lionheart, on his way to the Third Crusade (cf. above, p. 97). The Teutonic Knights, as has been seen (cf. above, p. 123) went first to Venice, the Order of St Lazarus to its commandery of Boigny in France, giving up en route the claim to be a military Order at all. But the Templars, the Hospitallers, and the Order of St Thomas of Acre – which claimed King Richard as its founder – moved their headquarters to the island. Though strategically well placed to launch further crusades against the Muslim occupiers of Palestine, it was a politically tricky location. It was difficult for the knights, suddenly present in such substantial numbers, to avoid becoming embroiled in the island's intrigues. Both the Hospital and, particularly, the Temple had substantial land holdings on Cyprus, in the case of the Templars of a size second only to those of the ruling family, the Lusignans. And relations between the Temple and the Lusignans had been fraught ever since, in the mid 1270s, the Templars had backed the Angevins rather than the Lusignans for the title of King of Jerusalem.

The military Orders had each its own way of dealing with the problems of

being located on Cyprus. From the 1320s the Order of St Thomas of Acre was trying to move its headquarters to London — which it succeeded in doing by the middle of the century. The Hospitallers decided to transfer from Cyprus to the island of Rhodes. They invaded Rhodes in 1306, but it was not until 1309 that they had finally overcome the resistance of that island's Greek Christian inhabitants — with whom from then on they struck up a relatively successful working relationship. The Templars stayed on Cyprus, and that perhaps contributed to their undoing.

At least the Hospitallers could present their occupation of Rhodes as preparing themselves to do battle once again against the infidel. To some contemporaries on the other hand the Templars appeared to be doing little for the crusade. That was unfair. They were gathering a fleet, and in 1306 their Grand Master, Jacques de Molay, submitted a report to the Pope calling for a new crusade, and setting out how it might be organized. His plan involved 15,000 knights and 50,000 foot soldiers being transported by sea to the Holy Land via the island of Cyprus. He also proposed a blockade of Egyptian trade. Molay's proposals were in response to Pope Clement V's request for advice. The Pope had also addressed the same request to the Master of the Hospital, Foulques de Villaret. He, too, was in favor of a blockade and, like de Molay, offered to commit his knights to enforce it. Molay, however, had added something to his report, which the Master of the Hospital thought it wiser to omit: Molay insisted there should be no amalgamation of the two Orders.

The suggestion that the two major military Orders should be somehow united to render them more effective, had been made several times in the last quarter of the thirteenth century. The proposal had many supporters. The Catalan (from Majorca) theologian Ramon Lull, who became a missionary to the Muslims and was stoned to death in Algeria in 1315, first proposed that, in order to avoid conflict between the Orders, each should be assigned a different front on which to fight. He eventually, however, came round to the opinion that they ought to be amalgamated. And that, said Pope Nicholas IV, who took soundings, was the general view.

De Molay was extremely hostile to any such move. Far from conflict between the Temple and the Hospital being a problem, he argued, the existence of two rather

Opposite: Town square and fountain, Rhodes

than one Order gave the crusaders a competitive edge. And if there were to be only one, how would it be decided who should go in front and who should constitute the rearguard: the Templars had traditionally ridden in the van.

Unfortunately for de Molay his chief adversary was to be not the sympathetic Pope Clement V but the unsympathetic King Philip II (the Fair) of France. Philip was in dire need of money. In 1306 he tried to reform the currency so as to improve the yield on the taxes levied by the Crown. His efforts were met with rioting — and he had to take refuge in the castle which served in Paris as the Templar treasury. As an alternative Philip seized the assets of Jews, arrested them, and expelled them from his kingdom. In 1307 he turned on the Templars. On 13 October that year all Templars throughout Philip's realm were arrested.

The charges laid against them were lurid, at least as John of Tour, the Templars' treasurer, confessed to them. When he was admitted, he told the papal inquisitor, he was shown a crucifix and told to spit on it, he was kissed by the knight who received him — on his back at the base of his spine, on his navel and on his lips. He was told that his vow of chastity prohibited sexual relations with women, but not with his fellow knights (though he insisted he had never seen acts of sodomy). He also suggested that the Templars secretly worshiped an idol.

It may be that Philip the Fair believed all this, though very few others did so. As well as being seriously short of funds Philip was also at the time in a state of heightened religious sensibility, fed by the death of his wife and the canonization in 1297 of his grandfather, the crusading King Louis IX. In that context he may have seen himself as protecting the honor of the crusading movement. If, that is, there were reasons to believe the accusations in the first place. But no secret statutes have ever been found, no idols. No evidence whatsoever has emerged of the Templars' guilt even though, under torture, members of the Order, including, on 24 October, Jacques de Molay himself, confessed to apostasy, to sodomy and to idolatry.

Pope Clement was furious at Philip's action. The Templars were under his protection, and he had not been consulted. But he had other problems. Philip was waging a campaign against Clement's predecessor in the papacy: the French King's assault on the Templars at least relieved that pressure. On 22 November Clement therefore ordered that all Templars throughout Christendom be arrested: only those in Aragón, where they holed up for a year in a castle, resisted. Philip then demanded that the Pope institute an inquiry into the Order. Again Clement conceded.

But as time went on it became increasingly evident that there was no substance to the accusations. Templars withdrew their confessions. That did not help them because then they were condemned as relapsed heretics, and relapsed heretics could be burnt at the stake. Fifty-four of them died that way at Paris on 12 May 1310. Philip was still not satisfied. He wanted a comprehensive condemnation by the Church of all the Templars and their doings. Clement V had little alternative but to agree, though the condemnation when it came, on 22 March 1312, just two days after a meeting between Philip and Clement, was only provisional, and did not accept the Templars' guilt. The Order was suppressed, its surviving members granted pensions, and its properties apart from those in the Iberian peninsular (cf. above, p. 152) were made over to the Hospitallers. If Philip had hoped to profit he was to be disappointed. His antipathy, however, had not yet been fully satisfied. After the suppression of the Templars Jacques de Molay and another senior member, both sentenced to life imprisonment, withdrew their confessions. They were burnt to death in Paris, on an island in the Seine, in March 1314.

Pope Clement V

THE CRUSADING SPIRIT COOLS

So great was the sudden increase in Hospitaller wealth through the demise of the Temple that the Order took some time to absorb it all. In London, where the Hospitallers already had their headquarters in Clerkenwell, they did not need the Templar church down by the Thames, and leased it out to lawyers. Templar estates in Cyprus passed immediately to the Hospital, those in France by 1318. This increased wealth the Hospitallers spent on Rhodes, building a hospital for pilgrims passing through, strengthening the castle, constructing the "auberges" for the different "langues" — they even eventually re-opened a hospital in Muslim-held Jerusalem.

But though after their General Chapter of 1311, held on Rhodes, they instituted a blockade of Egypt, the crusading endeavors of the Hospitallers declined in the fourteenth century. Partly this was because they were not led by men of distinction, partly it was because of money problems — either their own or those of the papacy. This reflected both the increased involvement of the Order with the papacy, and the decrease in revenue from priories, and this despite the flourishing trade it developed, sending the sugar it had grown westward, and importing eastward cloth to be sold on.

The drop in revenues reaching Rhodes was important, not just in monetary terms, but because of what it signified. As the crusading spirit grew colder, secular lords in the West were more insistent on taking taxes from Hospitaller lands. More worrying, however, was the fact that the priories were growing increasingly independent of the Convent on Rhodes. It was not just that responsions remained unpaid. The priories ignored attempts by the Master to reform the Order, by that means to forestall happening to the Hospitallers what had befallen the Templars: the Knights of Santiago for that very reason reformed themselves while the Templars were still on trial. It did not help their image, and their chances of survival, if the Hospitallers were not seen as active against the Turks; in 1355 the Pope of the day told the Hospitallers to take on the Turks or risk losing the Templar lands which had been ceded to them. In 1374 the Pope instructed them to take charge of the Christian-held port of Smyrna, which they did until it fell to the Mamluks in 1402. It was likewise involved in the defense of those parts of the Byzantine Empire that had not been recovered by the Byzantines in 1261.

In the second half of the fourteenth century the Hospitallers were indeed more active, taking part in various naval leagues of Christian states against the Mamluks. The Admiral of the Hospital fleet gradually came to rival even the Grand Master in prestige, though not until the second half of the fifteenth century. By that time Rhodes had been invested by the Mamluks three times, in 1440, in 1443, and in 1444. All these sieges had been beaten off by the Hospitallers, which did wonders for their morale. That the siege of 1480 was lifted despite the damage done to their defenses they greeted as a miracle, and built a church to celebrate. But they also strengthened their fortifications. The Hospitallers were now clearly on the front line: their Grand Master was rewarded with the cardinalate (in 1489), and the whole Order with the lands of the Orders of Saint Lazarus and the Holy Sepulchre.

In 1510 the Hospitallers won a major sea battle against the Mamluks, but the power of the Mamluks was in any case coming to an end. It was being challenged by a new Muslim dynasty, the Ottoman Turks. How and why the Ottomans, who came originally from the northwest corner of Anatolia, should have become such a force so rapidly in the Near East is difficult to explain. It may be that they were so ideally located in relation to the remnants of the Byzantine Empire that they attracted Islamic warriors who wished to wage holy war against the Christian state. It is unclear if the Ottomans were simply a band of warriors, or if they constituted a tribe, which drew such warriors to itself. But what is certain is that as a military force it emerged at the beginning of the fourteenth century, and swiftly expanded through Anatolia. By the end of the century the Ottomans had occupied Thrace and Macedonia. They then moved through the Balkans. In 1389 at Kosovo, on the "Field of Blackbirds", the Muslim army decisively defeated a Christian force made up of Albanians, Bosnians, Bulgars, Hungarians, Poles and Serbs under the Serbian King Lazarus. Before the battle the Ottoman sultan was assassinated with a poison dagger; after it King Lazarus was executed.

Throughout all this Constantinople remained in Christian hands. It was blockaded in 1394, but survived because the Ottomans were over-extended, fighting on two fronts. It was under siege again in 1422, but again held out. A third attempt to capture it began in 1451, this time with the help of artillery, much of it captured from European forces, or made for the Ottoman Turks by Christian gun-founders. And in 1453 Constantinople fell: the last Byzantine stronghold surrendered in 1460. Twenty years later Rhodes was under siege.

This time the Hospitallers' island, garrisoned by some 600 knights and sergeants, survived. Not only that but the story of the siege spread quickly around Europe, aided by the printing press. It brought the Knights of Rhodes new fame and fortune. And there was a respite from the fighting, for the Ottomans and the Mamluks now clashed. In the first round of the conflict the Mamluks were victorious but in the second, under the Ottoman Sultan Selim the Grim, the Mamluks were decisively defeated. The war, claimed Ottoman apologists, was a jihad, because the Mamluks were getting in the way of Selim attacking both the heretical Shi'as and the Christians. In 1517 the body of the last Mamluk sultan of Cairo was thrown over the gate of his city. The Ottomans were able once again to turn their attention to the Knights of Rhodes.

Rhodes was now encircled by the Ottomans, except to the west. It was of immense strategic importance because it lay across the path of naval links between Turkey and Egypt. It was inevitable that Suleyman the Magnificent, Ottoman sultan from 1520 to 1566, should lay siege to the Knights' stronghold. The siege began in mid-July 1521. Despite occasional intense fighting, and the execution for treason of the Hospitallers' Grand Chancellor, the 500 or so knights and the 1,500 soldiers from Rhodes itself held off the Turks until December. But their position was impossible. The Knights surrendered, and sailed from Rhodes for Italy and the papal states; the Grand Master was appointed Guardian of the conclave which in 1523 elected a member of the Order as Pope Clement VII.

For several years the Hospitallers were in search of a permanent home, though almost immediately after they left Rhodes the Emperor Charles V offered them the island of Malta. Charles needed all the support he could muster for the Ottomans were advancing steadily on his Empire. Belgrade had been captured in 1522; the Hungarians were defeated at the Battle of Mohacs in 1526. Three years later the Ottomans were at the gates of Vienna. Though Vienna survived the siege of 1529 it was evident that the Muslim army would be back. As adversaries of the Turks the Knights had an impressive reputation, but their retreat from Rhodes had left the Mediterranean far more open to Turkish galleys. Malta was the obvious place from which to mount a holding action. The Knights arrived there in June 1530 and immediately began to fortify the island.

Suleyman's fleet did not arrive off Malta until May 1565; the Turkish troops landed there on the nineteenth of that month. Under the Hospitaller Grand Master Jean de la Valette there were some 540 knights and sergeants, a small force of about 400 Spanish soldiers, and perhaps ten times that many Maltese to defend the island.

The Grand Harbour at Malta with St Elmo Fort at the end of the Peninsular

Valetta - fortifications. The Old Customs House adjoining Grand Harbour

There were 40,000 in the invading force. It was a bitter battle. First the Turks had to capture the castle of St Elmo, which controlled the entrance to the Grand Harbor. This took a month, at the end of which all the knights defending it were dead. The Turkish commander nailed the corpses to crosses, and floated them off in the harbor. In reply Jean de Valette decapitated all his Turkish prisoners, and fired their heads from canon into the Turkish camp. By September when relief arrived – led by a Commander of the Order of Santiago – well over 200 of the Knights, and perhaps as many as 5,000 other defenders, lay dead. The Turks abandoned their offensive on 8 September when the relief force landed. They did not realize until it was too late how small the force was.

The reputation of the Knights after their victory had rarely been higher. Its fame attracted new members. There were a great many recruits, though not all of the sort that brought honor to the Order. Jean de la Valette, who had fought at the siege of Rhodes before commanding at the siege of Malta, now began to build a new city, to which the name Valetta was given in his honor. It was to be well fortified. In 1614 there was a further Turkish landing, from a fleet of 60 galleys, but this time the invaders were more readily driven away.

In between the two invasions, on 7 October 1571, came the great naval battle in the Gulf of Corinth, the Battle of Lepanto. A fleet of the Catholic League, numbering some 200 galleys, faced about 275 Turkish ones. In all, perhaps as many as 100,000 men were involved on the two sides. The Knights could supply only three galleys – they had lost three the year before – but they were placed on the right wing. The Turkish fleet was driven on shore, and more than 30,000 of its crew were killed. Eighty Turkish galleys were destroyed, most of the rest captured. But the Knights suffered heavily, as they were put to fight the most skilful of the Turkish commanders. The crew of two of their galleys died almost to a man. Their leader survived, but with five arrows in his body. In his galley all but two of his knights had died, and the two had collapsed from their wounds. Around them were 300 Turkish dead. Unhappily, though the victory was much lauded in Europe, it proved to be fruitless. The League fell apart, Venice once again proving itself an unreliable ally, while the Turks replaced their destroyed or captured fleet with extraordinary rapidity, building galleys at an average of one a day.

The Muslim advance within Europe had not yet reached its climax. That came in 1683 with the final attempt to take Vienna. Under the King of Poland, John Sobieski, Christian forces defeated those of Islam, and the long withdrawal of the Ottomans from Europe began. In 1699, at the Treaty of Karlowitz, the Turks ceded Hungary and Transylvania to Austria. A former

John Sobieski, King of Poland

Knight Hospitaller who had become a priest and then a bishop, and who had been active in encouraging Christians in defense of Vienna during its siege was, even before the 1699 Treaty, declared Prince Primate of Hungary.

In the Reformation the Knights Hospitaller, though some of their priories were dissolved (that of England, for example, in 1540), for the most part retained their Catholic allegiance, and their commanderies. In 1700 there were still 560 scattered across Europe. One commandery that did not remain Catholic was the priory of Brandenburg where many of the Knights embraced Protestantism. This priory nonetheless continued in existence, though as a Lutheran Order; in the late eighteenth century it re-established links with the Order's headquarters on Malta.

THE TEUTONIC KNIGHTS

The story of the Teutonic Knights, on the other hand, was much more fragmented. The Order itself effectively divided in two, the Knights in Livonia electing their own Master, and going their own way, from the middle of the fifteenth century. Many of the problems of the Teutonic Order, and especially of those in Prussia, were of their own making. It faced constant hostility from Poland, and its need to hire mercenaries – by the middle of the fifteenth century there were at any one time only some 200 Knights in Prussia – made its finances increasingly difficult to manage. It paid its way through trade – and that became more problematic as England and Holland developed in competition – and by taxing the countryside over which it ruled. Taxation led to unrest. The harshness of its regime alienated the people of Prussia. The Estates, a form of government involving the local population which was established by the Order in an attempt to appear less autocratic, united against them, and, not surprisingly Poland gave its support to the federation of the Estates. War broke out in 1454, and the Knights suffered a series of defeats. In 1466, at the Second Treaty of Thorn, the Knights were obliged to cede much of their territory to Poland and to agree to hold the remainder as a fief of the Polish King. Their castle of Marienburg was abandoned,

The Battle of Lepanto

and a new headquarters established at Königsberg in East Prussia. In 1497, therefore, it was as a vassal of the Polish King that the Grand Master led a force of 4,000 into battle against the Turks who were threatening Poland.

In Livonia the economy was more flourishing, and the 200 or so Knights appeared less menacing to the Livonian population. Their battles were against the Orthodox of Novgorod, and then of Moscow. After a visit to Martin Luther in 1523 the Grand Master of the whole Order became a Protestant, and two years later the Order in Prussia was dissolved. In Livonia, however, the Knights remained Catholic and the Order survived, at least for a few more years. Its eventual nemesis was Ivan the Terrible. The Tsar invaded Livonia in 1558, and laid it waste. The defeated Teutonic Knights of Livonia secularized their Order three years later. In both Prussia and Livonia the Master became an hereditary Duke.

For Teutonic knights living outside Prussia and Livonia the situation was different. Some of the German commanderies remained Catholic, and survived. For these new rules were drawn up in 1606, which obliged recruits to three years service on the Turkish front. Individual Knights had eminent careers in the service of the Empire and elsewhere, and in 1696 the Order established its own regiment. The last Knight to be Grand Master became in 1916 a field marshal in the Austro-Hungarian army. After that the Teutonic Order, which had always of course included priests and nuns, became purely religious, engaged in pastoral and charitable work. In that manner it still survives.

THE IBERIAN ORDERS

The history of the Iberian Orders was very different. That of the Order of Avis was the oddest. In 1385 its Grand Master seized the throne of Portugal and founded a new dynasty – that of Avis. He annexed the Order to the Crown, and instructed that henceforward the head of the Order should be a member of the royal family. The chaplains of the Order, however, survived as a religious body until the secularization of all the Orders in 1834. The Order of Christ suffered a similar fate. It, too, was taken over by the crown though not until the middle of the sixteenth century – the Infante Henry the Navigator was Administrator of the Order. The Orders of Christ, of Avis, and of St James of the Sword finally became ranks of honor in Portugal, bestowed by the crown on those judged worthy recipients of an order of chivalry.

In Spain, even before the conquest of Granada, the Catholic kings had indicated that they would reserve the Mastership of the Orders to the Crown. The Order of Montesa, technically in the Kingdom of Valencia, managed to retain its independence until 1588, when it was annexed to the crown of Aragón, but as early as the year after the fall of Granada the Spanish Crown took over the running of the Orders of Calatrava, Santiago and of Alcántara. The Council of the Orders was established in 1494. In 1523 Pope Adrian VI, who had once been tutor to the Emperor Charles V, approved the Emperor's proposal to incorporate the Orders into the Crown of Spain. In 1540 the requirement that the professed Knights should remain celibate was removed. Some years later King Philip II ordered Calatrava to break off all ties with the Cistercians.

By taking over the Orders the Crown of Spain laid hands on immense wealth. It also gave Spanish monarchs the opportunity to bestow the titles of Knight on people they wanted somehow to honor: among the approximately 13,000 made Knights of Santiago between the beginning of the sixteenth century and the end of the nineteenth, there were several of the Conquistadores of the Americas. Another was Don John of Austria, victor of the Battle of Lepanto. There were benefits to knighthood. The Orders continued rigorously to insist upon nobility, and legitimacy, of birth, and on purity of blood – no one from a family that had once been either Jewish or Muslim could be a member. Therefore to be admitted to one of the Orders was a sign to the world of the family's distinguished status, and as such was much prized.

Individual members of these Orders may have had distinguished careers, military and administrative, but the Orders as such ceased to take the field as a body, though the conquest of the New World might have provided an opportunity. It was because of war in the Americas that theologians turned back to the issue of holy war, and of just war. This became a subject much debated by scholars in the sixteenth century, among them the Dominican Francisco de Vitoria who died in 1546.

The question arose whether the Spaniards had any right at all to be in America.

Were the conquistadores not simply depriving the native peoples of their rightful property? Everyone agreed, along with Aquinas, that it was not enough to say that, if someone was not a Christian, therefore he did not enjoy the right to ownership of property: "It is obviously unjustifiable to seize the possessions of Saracens, Jews or other infidels, simply because they are infidels," Aquinas had earlier laid down; "it is just as much an act of theft or robbery as it would be if it were done to Christians." Similarly the indigenous population of the Americas had a right to their land simply because they were in possession of it; their society had as much right to ownership of it by natural law, argued Vitoria, as individuals had to their own bits and pieces of property — basically because they needed it to survive. In this argument Vitoria even included mineral and fishing rights, pointing out that the kings of Spain and Portugal claimed as much for their own dominions, so why not the native peoples for theirs.

Nor, he went on, could the conquest be justified on the grounds simply of spreading Christianity; if the natives refused to obey God, some people insisted, war could be waged against them until they were forced to convert. Vitoria was having none of that. They could not be forced to accept Christianity "unless there have been miracles or some other proof," he said. A refusal to be converted, in other words, was no justification for making war on the Indians. There could not be for Christians, he was arguing, such a thing as holy war, a war of conversion.

More problematic was the argument that the conquistadores were justified in making war on the Indians because of the latter's obnoxious practices, such as cannibalism. But is this any more of a sin than is either adultery or fornication, asks Vitoria, yet no one would say that a ruler may go to war with another ruler so as to stop adultery happening. However, despite this argument, Vitoria does in fact think a Christian monarch can go to war to stop human sacrifice and cannibalism, because in doing so he is protecting the innocent.

So what is the mandate for colonizing the Americas? It is, in effect, trusteeship. Lands may be taken over for the welfare and benefit of the natives, but certainly not simply for the profit of Spain and Portugal.

Vitoria believed that the Spaniards' right to go to war on the American Indians, in so far as it existed at all, was severely limited; it turned on the right, believed to exist in natural law, to travel, to trade and to settle. If such rights were forcibly denied, they might be forcibly defended but, he said, only if the good which will arise as a consequence of the war outweighs the harm which will be done by going to war. It was Vitoria who, in the middle of the sixteenth century, and in the context of the conquest of the Americas, added to the theory of the just war the concept of proportionality – that a war is just only if the good achieved is greater than the damage done.

When Vitoria was writing down his thoughts on the justice of warfare the era of the crusades as it is normally understood was long over. Though there was still war between the Muslim Ottomans and the Christian European states, by then it could certainly be portrayed – even perhaps on the Baltic where Catholics confronted Orthodox – as war undertaken in self-defense, the only legitimate kind of war. And by Vitoria's day the story of the military religious Orders was all but over. The only one still surviving as an effective fighting force was the Hospitallers of St John of Jerusalem, who were soon to become known more popularly as the Knights of Malta.

TWISTS AND TURNS

In Malta the Knights gradually established a sovereign state. After the 1565 siege the enhancement of the island's fortifications continued for the next two centuries. At the beginning of the seventeenth century recruitment was high. The Knights' galleys continued to patrol the Mediterranean, in regular conflict with Muslim corsairs, and the Knights even occasionally mounted expeditions against Muslim-held territory. Again during the first half of the eighteenth century numbers rose. Early in the eighteenth century the Order built large sailing vessels, ships-of-the-line, to accompany their galleys. At the end of that century the Knights' fleet included two ships-of-the-line, alongside four galleys and two frigates. There were by then over 300 Knights living on Malta, two-thirds of them French.

But France itself, at the Revolution, turned against the Knights as it did against the Church as a whole. In 1792 the National Assembly stripped the Knights of their French possessions. In the wars that followed the Revolution the Order lost its estates in Germany, Switzerland and Italy. And then, in 1798, Napoleon expelled the Grand Master and surviving Knights from Malta itself with scarcely a shot being fired.

There followed one of the more bizarre incidents in the long history of the Order. In a desperate search for a new home the Knights turned to Tsar Paul I of Russia, who in 1798 was elected Grand Master – despite the fact that he was not a professed member, or even a Catholic. Just over two years later, however, Tsar Paul was assassinated, and his successor laid no claim to the Order, which, in 1834, finally found a permanent home in Rome.

Even before then the French "langue", always the most numerous in the Order, had reconstituted itself – though effectively as independent of the Grand Master – and was romantically planning once more to take on the Ottoman Empire, now in terminal decline but still a significant force. There were plans to re-establish the Knights on Rhodes, even to regain the Holy Land. For this the French Knights turned for help to England, and an Order of St John was established in Britain, originally to raise money for these schemes. The plans came to nothing but the Order established in England, as the Order now based in Rome, turned to charitable activities, especially ambulance services. The St John Ambulance Brigade was an offshoot.

In Rome the Knights survived, and still survive, as a Catholic religious Order. They constitute a sovereign Order, though a sovereign without a territory. There are a few professed knights, about 40 in all, who still take the three vows and live, wherever there are enough of them, a semblance of a conventual life. These are now called Knights of Justice. Associated with them is a very much larger group, Knights (and Dames) of Honor and Devotion, who support and manage ambulance services, hospitals, medical centers, and orphanages around the world. Such activities are presented as a return to the original purpose of the Hospitallers as the Order came into being in the early twelfth century.

But however laudable such activities, they are a long way removed from the story for which the Knights Hospitallers are most remembered. They, together with the Templars, the Teutonic Knights, the Knights of St Thomas of Acre and St Lazarus, fought in the twelfth and thirteenth centuries to preserve the Holy Places of Palestine in Christian hands. In that they were unsuccessful. It is doubtful whether they even held up, or held up for long, the progress of the forces of Islam from Asia Minor to central Europe.

In the Iberian peninsular the Orders of Knighthood had more success. There, with local levies and occasional crusading expeditions from France (neither in Spain nor in the Holy Land did the Orders themselves constitute the larger part of the Christian forces), they managed to drive the Moslems back to North Africa. As has been seen, the final Muslim Kingdom, Granada, fell to Ferdinand and Isabella in 1492. It was in that year, too, that Columbus sailed, with the backing of the Spanish monarchs, in the voyage that led to the discovery of the Americas. One cannot but wonder what might have happened had the Christians not triumphed in Spain. Might it have been that the galleys that crossed the Atlantic in 1492 would have been crewed by Muslim sailors, and Muslim warriors? Might the New World have been colonized by conquistadores whose religion was Islam rather than Christianity?

But for the victories of the Knights of Calatrava, or Alcántara and Santiago, of Montesa and Avis, and of the Hospitallers, the world could have been a very different place.

Appendix 1

The Templar Myth

Jacques de Molay, the last Grand Master of the Templars, as technically a relapsed heretic, was burnt at the stake in Paris on 19 March 1314. Pope Clement V, who had, albeit unwillingly, abetted Philip the Fair in his efforts to suppress the Templars, died just a month later, on 20 April. The French King himself died in an accident on 29 November that same year. The reasons for suppressing the Order had been spurious: most people who thought about it at all were agreed. The deaths of the two chief persecutors of Jacques de Molay within nine months of his execution — was it a curse?

The crimes with which the Templars had been charged were both salacious and blasphemous: the possibilities of the Templar story were endless, and in the seven centuries since much has been, and continues to be, made of them. In his fascinating little book *The Murdered Magicians* (Oxford University Press, 1982), Peter Partner traces the literary tradition of the Templar myth back to what was little more than a passing remark in the *De Occulta Philosophia* ('On the secret [or hidden] philosophy') of Heinrich Cornelius Agrippa von Nettesheim (1486–1535). Agrippa was a writer, a soldier, a physician and, by common repute, a magician, whose varied career including teaching theology in Cologne and serving the Emperor Charles V as historian and archivist. Although the book was not published until 1531, the text of *De Occulta Philosophia* was probably written c. 1510, when Agrippa was in Cologne. He argues in this influential text that it is by magic — which he interprets very broadly — that people may come to know the nature of God. He associates the obscene rituals of which the Templars were accused — though he rather suggests that the charges were doubtful — with magic. His prudent doubts were not always shared by others who read his book.

An alternative vision of the Templars was promoted by the French Catholic politician and political philosopher Jean Bodin (1530–1596), who put them alongside the Jews as unjustly oppressed by Philip the Fair.

It was with the development of Freemasonry that the Templar myth reached its height. Myth-making was encouraged by the fact that very little is known of the origins of Freemasonry before the foundation of the Premier Grand Lodge in London in 1717. The notion that it had anything to do with crusaders comes, however, not from London but from Paris, and in particular from the speculations of a Jacobite exile in France, Andrew Michael Ramsay. Ramsay was a Roman Catholic — Catholics were not yet forbidden to be members of the Masons — who had been secretary to François Fénelon, a philosopher and theologian, preacher and spiritual guide, and man about the French royal court until one of his books was thought to criticize Louis XIV and he was banished back to the diocese of Cambrai where he was Archbishop. For his services to Fénelon — he was also his literary executor — Ramsay was rewarded with a knighthood, that of St Lazarus, and was from then on known as the Chevalier Ramsay.

Ramsay's interest in the crusades may have been sparked by his title. Whatever the reason, in 1737, when he had become Chancellor of the Grand Lodge in France, he had proposed a link between Freemasonry and the crusaders in the Holy Land (not specifically the Templars), who recognized each other in a hostile environment by the exchange of secret signs. Ramsay's purpose in all this was to introduce a new and exotic element into Masonry, which had hitherto

The burning of Jacques de Molay

limited itself to the three basic levels, or degrees, of membership: Entered Apprentice, Fellow Craft and Master Mason, supposedly derived from the guilds, or lodges, of medieval stonemasons. In keeping with a growing desire for titles of nobility by which the growing bourgeoisie could be assimilated in a controlled way into the aristocracy, Ramsay wanted to introduce titles of knighthood into the Masons.

There was also an occult element to Ramsay's discourse. The crusaders, he suggested, had associated in Jerusalem with the masons of the Temple of Solomon. These masons had mystic knowledge, which they willingly handed on to the crusaders. This knowledge had survived, claimed the Chevalier, because some of the crusaders had, on their return home, established lodges where these mysteries were handed on. All such lodges had long died out – except, it was claimed, in England and Scotland.

Masonic scales

Ramsay's baseless speculations did not link the Masons specifically to the Templars. That happened shortly afterwards in Germany, where it was proposed that the secret knowledge which the Templars possessed came not from the masons of the Temple of Solomon but from the Essenes, a Jewish sect which was roughly contemporary with Christ (John the Baptist is sometimes said to have been an Essene). The Essenes had long died out, and indeed very little was then known of them, though a great deal more has been discovered since especially through the Dead Sea Scrolls. But the air of mystery about them made it easier to propound the notion that they were bearers of a secret knowledge. This knowledge they had handed on, went the theory, to the Canons of the Church of the Holy Sepulchre, and hence to the Templar Grand Masters. Jacques de Molay had passed this knowledge on before his death. He

had also sent his nephew to rescue the Templar treasures, which included the crown of the Kingdom of Jerusalem, and the seven-branched candlestick which in 70CE had been taken from the Temple by the Roman General, and future Emperor, Titus.

The Temple of Solomon

This farrago of nonsense took hold of German Freemasonry, was adopted with alacrity in America, and eventually made its way to Britain. Templar Masonry still flourishes, especially in the United States, where its ruling body is known rather romantically as "the Grand Encampment".

Though the notion of a secret knowledge possessed by the Templars became widespread, not all those who subscribed to the belief were sympathetic. The Abbé Augustin Barruel published his three-volume *Mémoires pour servir l'histoire du Jacobinisme* in 1797–98 when he was in exile in London. In it he argued that secret societies were behind the French Revolution, which had driven him out of France. But these secret societies, among which were of course the Masons, were the heirs of a long tradition of subversive movements. Among these movements were numbered the Albigensians and the Templars. Barruel was a former member of the Society of Jesus, the Jesuits, whom some had accused of backing the Masons and therefore being behind the Revolution. In 1773 when the Jesuits were suppressed by the Pope of the day, the suppression of the Templars was produced as a precedent.

The Holy Grail

Barruel was a loyal Jesuit — he returned to the Society of Jesus when it was reestablished in 1815 — and had no love for the Templars, who in any case played only a small part in his overall thesis. Nevertheless the idea caught on that they were part of a long tradition of anarchist movements. It is to be found again in Joseph von Hammer-Purgstall's (who began life rather more simply as Joseph Hammer) *Mystery of Baphomet Revealed* of 1818. Baphomet meant "baptism of the spirit", claimed Hammer — it was actually the medieval French name for Muhammad — and it was the idol that the Templars were accused of worshipping. They also worshipped, and were guardians of, the Holy Grail, said Hammer, but this had no Christian meaning. Instead of it being, as in most stories, the cup out of which Christ drank at the Last Supper, the Grail, said Hammer, was a symbol of the Gnostics, and of a special brand of Gnostics who had cursed Christ. Hammer's views appealed to the Austrian statesman Metternich for whom he worked — the idea of there being a long history of secret radicalism served to bolster his own conservative policies.

Another propagator of similar ideas was Gabriele Rossetti. Rossetti was father of the poet and painter Dante Gabriel Rossetti, and himself a poet as well as being, after his exile from Italy in 1820, professor of Italian at the newly established University College in London. In 1832 he published a book in which he claimed to have found a whole string of anti-papal and heretical movements in the Middle Ages, among them the Templars. Rossetti, however, approved of such radicalism.

In Paris this spurious history even gave rise to a kind of church, whose doctrines were believed to have been handed down by Templar Grand Masters who had received them from the Patriarch of Jerusalem, who had in turn got them from the Gnostics. This sect even invented a calendar based on the date of the foundation of the Knights Templar in 1118.

They could claim the line of descent of the Grand Masters because in 1804 a document was discovered which listed them all from Jacques de Molay onwards. And they had all conveniently signed it. This was an obvious forgery, but a glance at web sites of modern "Knights Templar" will readily show that it is still believed.

Napoleon, who had more than a passing interest in the Templars himself, had papal archives moved to Paris in 1810, where the proceedings against the Templars were studied. No evidence was found to support the charges against them, therefore no evidence of salacious and blasphemous practices, but nor was there evidence entirely to exonerate them. The case remained not proven. A distinguished historian, Jean Michelet, edited the Templar trials, but he believed they might have been influenced by the doctrines of Eastern sects and therefore deviated from Catholic orthodoxy. His failure to endorse their innocence affected later historians who were indebted to his work.

The Emperor Napoleon

There were more forgeries. Two secret rules were discovered and published in 1877, one of them indecent.

The nineteenth-century passion for medieval knighthoods was well represented in literature, in art, in music. In Britain Sir Walter Scott portrayed the Templars in two novels, *Ivanhoe* and *The Talisman*, in both instances as villains. He was much more sympathetic to the Hospitallers. The attempt to start an English branch of the Knights Hospitallers has been mentioned (cf. above, p. 185). There was, however, also a move to restart the Knights Templar in England. The leading spirit was Admiral Sir Sidney Smith who, in 1799, had been engaged in putting down an insurrection of Turkish Janissaries in Cyprus. For this he was rewarded by the Archbishop with a cross, which, said the Archbishop, had been left behind in a church by Richard I when he captured the island. Smith wanted his Knights to be,

Sir Walter Scott

once again, a military force operating in the Mediterranean. Nothing came of it.

In the late nineteenth and early twentieth century English folklorists were much taken with the idea of the Holy Grail, and Templar involvement, and this kept the myths very much alive and gave them the appearance of scholarly respectability. It has frequently been fuelled by legends of the Templars' hidden wealth. Ian Wilson, in his book on the supposed relic of Christ known as the Shroud of Turin, claims that the Templars owned it between it being taken from Constantinople in 1204 and its reappearance again in private possession towards the end of the fourteenth century.

And then there is *Foucault's Pendulum*, the second novel of the Italian professor of semiotics, Umberto Eco. On his own web site, Eco describes this book as follows:

> It is a well where fact mingles almost imperceptibly with fiction, where secret societies chart the true course of human evolution, and the occult exerts its subversive influence on reality in ways barely glimpsed by the average individual. Here the Templars and the Illuminati trade secrets in the darkened house of ignorance, and the lightbearers are only as trusty as their Ur-father Lucifer.
>
> Or it could all be an illusion.

Appendix 2

The Military Religious Orders

Below are listed the military religious Orders, with a brief account of each, for the most part as they are described in the *Dizionario degli Istituti dei Perfezione*. The list is as near as possible complete, but it does not include descriptions of the female branches of these Orders, of which there were several. It also does not include purely honorific papal, and other, knighthoods.

Alcántara, Order of, founded c. 1160–1170 under the name of the Order of Saint Julián de Pereiro, Pereiro being on the frontier between Portugal and the Kingdom of León. It seems to have at first been wholly monastic — its head is designated in the earliest documents as the "prior" but later becomes the "Master". It received papal confirmation in 1177. Its rule and structure mirrored that of Calatrava. When in 1218 Calatrava was given the castle of Alcántara, it made the fortress over to San Julián de Pereiro, and the Order then took the name of castle for its title. Its later history also followed that of Calatrava.

Aubrac, Order of, basically an Order of Hospitallers, though with a few knights, originally intended to safeguard from marauders the hospital for pilgrims to Rome and Compostella. It takes its name from its location, in the diocese of Rodez in France, and its rule was approved by the Bishop of Rodez in 1162. The number of knights was never large, but the Knights Hospitallers made a number of attempts to annex Aubrac.

It remained independent, however, until the French Revolution, when it ceased to exist.

Avis, Order of, possibly began as a confraternity of knights. As a military Order it is first recorded in 1167, when its members lived in the Portuguese city of Evora which had just been conquered from the Muslims. It linked with the Order of Calatrava in 1187, though it remained independent. Hitherto its members had followed the rule of St Benedict, but after the link with Calatrava it acknowledged the spiritual authority of the Cistercian abbey of Morimond. In 1223 its main location was moved to Avis. In 1385 its Grand Master seized the Portuguese throne and established the Avis dynasty: henceforward it was under the command of a member of the royal house. The chaplains survived as an Order until the secularization of the religious Orders in 1834: the rank of knighthood became entirely honorific.

Bethlehem, Order of Our Lady of: there were two military Orders with this name. The earlier, in the time of the crusades, was under the jurisdiction of the Bishop of Bethlehem and was formally known as the Military Order of the Crusaders of the Red Star. Very little is known of this Order, and certainly nothing of its military activity. On the other hand it had hospitals in Bohemia, France, Italy, and Britain. The one in London, founded in 1247, was that of St Mary of Bethlehem (Bedlam). The hospital in Scotland, in St Andrews, was even earlier (1219): it was taken over by the University in 1277. The later Bethlehemites were founded in 1459 by Pope Pius II specifically to defend the island of Lemnos, which had recently been captured from the Turks. It was endowed with the estates of several Orders, including that of St Lazarus. The Turks, however, promptly retook Lemnos, and the Order came to a sudden end.

Calatrava, Order of, founded in 1158 by the abbot Raymund Serrat of the Cistercian abbey of Fitero. Its purpose was to defend the castle of Calatrava, which controlled access to Toledo from the South. The General Chapter of Citeaux accepted it as part of the Cistercians in 1187 and placed it under the jurisdiction of the abbey of Morimond. Both knights and

The castle of Calatrava

chaplains were, technically, monks. Something of the history of the Order is given above (p. 182). It was annexed to the Crown in 1482, an action approved by the pope in 1523. It was distinctive in that it had not demanded from its knights evidence of noble birth. It was suppressed by the Spanish government in 1835, but re-established in the diocese named "the Priory of the Orders" (Ciudad Real) in 1851, though this was itself suppressed by the government in 1931.

Christ of Livonia, Order of Knights of, see Sword Brethren

Christ, Order of, founded in Portugal, and approved by a papal bull, in 1319, to take over the property of the Knights Templar after their suppression. It was located at Castro Marim, though it later occupied Tomar, the Templars' chief castle in Portugal. It adopted the rule of the Order of Calatrava, but put itself under the spiritual direction of the Cistercian abbey of Alcobaça. It was brought under the Portuguese crown in 1551 and became purely honorific (the senior Portuguese honor), though the chaplains continued to live a monastic life at Tomar until the secularization of the Orders in 1834. An Italian branch of the Order became the supreme honorific Order of Knighthood of the Holy See.

Constantinian Order, see George of Parma, Order of Saint

Dobrin, Order of, founded in 1228 by the Cistercian Bishop Christian of Prussia and Duke Corrado of Masovia, and approved by the pope the same year. Its purpose was to defend Masovia from the incursions of the pagan Prussians. It took its name from the Castle of Dobrin (Dobrzyn) on the Vistula. It was given all rights over the surrounding territories. In 1235 it was incorporated into the Teutonic Knights and, though the incorporation was resisted for a time, the Order had disappeared by 1240.

George of Alfama, Order of Saint, founded by King Peter I of Aragón in 1201. Peter had a particular devotion to St George, hence the title, and the castle that served as the Order's headquarters was at Alfama, on the coast between Tortosa and Tarragona. It followed the same rule of St Augustine as did the Knights Hospitallers, though the rule was not formally approved by the papacy until 1372. At that point it had six members. It was amalgamated with the Order of Montesa in 1400.

George of Carinthia, Order of Saint, founded jointly by the Emperor Frederic III and Pope Paul II in 1469 to defend the Empire against the incursions of Islam. It was based at the castle of Millstatt, a former monastery whose property was the first endowment of the Order. The Order had both military and charitable endeavors, and followed the rule of the Teutonic Knights. Members took vows of chastity and obedience, but not of poverty, keeping their own possessions, though they lived a communal life. It proved extremely difficult to attract recruits, and though it survived to the end of the sixteenth century it was of little significance. It was suppressed in 1598 and its property given to the Jesuits. A group claiming to descend from Saint George of Carinthia still exists with Millstatt as its spiritual home, but it is not a religious Order.

George of Parma, Order of Saint, sometimes called the Constantinian Order in the belief that it was founded by the Emperor Constantine in the fourth century AD. The first documents that can be dated with any certainty, however, date from 1522. These indicate that it was an Order of knighthood. It settled at Parma in 1697.

Hospitallers, the name most commonly used throughout this book for what is now properly entitled The Sovereign Military and Hospitaller Order of St John of Jerusalem, called of Rhodes, called of Malta. This is still a religious Order in the Roman Catholic Church, with professed Knights and chaplains. The Knights who are professed, a fairly small number, are entitled Knights of Justice; there are also married members called Knights (or Dames) of Honor and Devotion. The Hospitallers arose to serve the hospital provided in Jerusalem by merchants from Amalfi, and first achieved the status of a religious Order under Brother Gerard in the aftermath of the conquest of Jerusalem. The Brothers followed the rule of St Augustine, and were approved in 1113. The date at which they developed their military capability is uncertain, but it was certainly well established by

A Knight Hospitaller of St John of Jerusalem

the 1180s. After the fall of Acre in 1291 the Order transferred first to Cyprus, then to Rhodes (1310) and in 1530 to Malta, having been driven out of Rhodes by the forces of Suleyman the Magnificent in 1523. It was driven from Malta by Napoleon in 1798, and settled in Rome in 1834. In Malta it had established a sovereign state, and the Hospitallers still claim sovereign status. It is now engaged in charitable work such as providing ambulances and hospitals.

James of Altopascio, Order of Saint, founded at Altopascio near Lucca in Italy, possibly by the Countess Matilda of Canossa, between 1070 and 1080. It was originally an Order of Hospitallers, probably following the Augustinian rule. Its purpose was to provide care for pilgrims to Rome or to the Holy Land, and later those to the shrine of St James at Compostella in Spain. The military aspect of the Order developed later, on the model of the other military Orders, not to fight in the Holy Land but to keep down bandits and protect pilgrims. It spread across much of Europe in the twelfth and thirteenth centuries. It was suppressed in 1459, and its property passed to the Order of Our Lady of Bethlehem, which was founded in the same year. The Bull of suppression was not however implemented everywhere. It was subsequently suppressed in Italy in 1587, and its Italian property transferred to the Order of St Stephen, and in France in 1672, when its property was handed to the Order of St Lazarus.

James of the Sword, Order of Saint, see Santiago, Order of

James, Order of Saint, see Santiago, Order of

Jesus Christ, Order of Knights of, founded in Parma in 1233 by the Dominican Bartolomeo of Vicenza, and approved the following year by the pope. Its members, all nobles, did not live a communal life, or take a vow of poverty. They were committed to defending the Catholic faith against heretics. Their spiritual guidance was provided by members of the Dominican Order. They went out of existence in 1261 when their property was transferred to the Order of the Blessed and Glorious Virgin Mary.

Jesus Christ, Order of Knights of the Faith of, founded in the Languedoc to combat the Albigensians (Cathars). It came into being about the year 1218, and received papal approval in 1221. It followed the Augustinian rule, but had no links with any other religious Order. Its purpose ceased in 1229 with the reconciliation to the Church of Count Raymond VI of Toulouse and Duke Aimeric of Narbonne. Its members affiliated with the Order of Saint James of the Sword.

John of Jerusalem, Order of Saint, see Hospitallers

Julián de Pereiro, Order of Saint, see Alcántara, Order of

Lazarus, Order of Saint, founded in Jerusalem c. 1120 to care for the sick, especially lepers. Like the Knights Hospitallers it followed the rule of St Augustine. Also like the Hospitallers, from its care for the sick it developed a company of Brother Knights, and at about the same time (c. 1180). Its main residence in the West was at Boigny-les-Barres near Orleans, which became its headquarters after the fall of Acre in 1291. From then on it abandoned any military role. In 1489 Pope Innocent VIII tried to amalgamate it with Knights Hospitallers, but this was rejected except by members in Germany, and remaining property, except that in France, was handed to the Order of St Maurice in 1572. In France Henry IV wanted to reconstitute the Order of St Lazarus, but the Pope was hesitant. Henry therefore created a new Order, that of Our Lady of Mount Carmel, which received papal approval in 1608. Henry then appointed to head the new Order the already existing Grand Master of the Order of St Lazarus, and the two were effectively combined under the name of Our Lady of Mount Carmel and of Saint Lazarus of Jerusalem. It was purely honorific, and was abolished at the Revolution.

Malta, Knights of, see Hospitallers

Mary, Order of the Blessed and Glorious Virgin, founded at Bologna by Loderengo Andalb, and approved by a papal bull in 1261. Its members were vowed to live an exemplary life, and to conjugal chastity. They undertook various works of charity, particularly of widows and orphans. The knights were further committed to maintain peace in their region. The Order spread to various Italian cities, but gradually went into decline, surviving in Bologna itself until 1589 and in Treviso to 1737.

Mary of Spain, Order of Saint, founded by King Alfonso X of Castile in 1272, or

Cartagena, headquarters of the Order of St Mary of Spain

possibly slightly earlier, as a maritime Order: its houses were at Cartagena (the headquarters), San Sebastián, La Coruña and Puerto de Santa María. It followed the rule adopted by the Order of Calatrava, and was an affiliate of the Cistercian abbey of Granselve, in France. It did not have great success, and its remit was extended to land warfare. In 1281, after the Order of Santiago had lost a very large number of knights in the battle of Moclín the year before, it was merged with Santiago, and ceased to exist as an independent Order.

Maurice, Order of Saint, founded by Amadeus VIII of Savoy in 1434, and refounded in 1572. It followed the Cistercian rule. Members took the vows of obedience and of conjugal chastity, they swore obedience to the pope, and acceptance of the decrees of the Council of Trent, which had just concluded. Though entirely dependent on the House of Savoy, its avowed purpose was the defense of the papacy.

Mercedarians (Order of Our Lady of Mercy for the Redemption of Captives) founded in Barcelona in 1218 by Peter Nolasco. It was approved by the pope in 1235. It followed the rule of St Augustine. Its purpose was to rescue Christian slaves from captivity among the Muslims. It was at first a primarily military Order, though the clerics grew in number, and the knights declined. A disputed election for Master General held at Puig in Valencia in 1317 led to clerical dominance. The knights then joined the newly founded Order of Montesa. The Mercedarians still exist, though as a purely clerical religious Order.

Monte Gaudio, Order of, named after the hill near Jerusalem (Montjoie, Mountjoy) from which pilgrims first caught sight of the city, founded after 1171 by Rodrigo Alvarez, count of Sarriá, who had left the Order of Santiago. The affiliation of the Order with that of Cîteaux was approved in 1180. Rodrigo died in 1186 and there was an attempt made to amalgamate with the Knights Templar. Some members became Templars in 1196, but others settled at the castle of Montfragüe, in Castile, and took its name before in 1221 uniting with the Order of Calatrava, thus bringing Calatrava into dispute with the Templars. The issue was not settled finally, in favor of Calatrava, until 1245. Further details can be found in the text, pp. 135-137.

Montesa, Order of, founded by James II of Aragón to receive the property in his kingdom of the Knights Templar. It was approved by a bull of 1317, though it was not formed until two years later. It took its name from a castle in the kingdom of Valencia which had belonged to the Templars. It adopted the rule of Calatrava, and was under the spiritual guidance of the Cistercian monastery of Santas Creus in Catalonia. When the Mercedarians became a purely clerical Order, its knights joined Montesa. The knights of St George of Alfama likewise joined in 1400. It was incorporated into the Crown of Aragón in 1587. A diocese-priory was created in 1851 for all the Spanish Orders at Ciudad Real, which survived until the Spanish Civil War.

Montfragüe, Order of, see Monte Gaudio

Montjoie (Mountjoy), Order of, see Monte Gaudio

Montmorillon, Order of, founded at Montmorillon in the diocese of Poitiers in 1086 by Robert du Puy, seemingly on his return from the Holy Land. It main purpose was to run a hospital, but it was also to look after pilgrims to Jerusalem, and the poor of the region. It had in addition the task of recruiting knights for the crusade. The rule was that of St Augustine. In 1562 the house of the Order was sacked by Protestants, and abandoned.

Mount Carmel, Our Lady of and Saint Lazarus of Jerusalem, see Lazarus, Order of Saint

Rhodes, Knights of, see Hospitallers

Santiago, Order of, founded in 1170 by Ferdinand II of León at Cáceres in Estremadura as a confraternity of knights. The following year it undertook to safeguard a lordship of the Archbishop of Santiago de Compostella which was close to Cáceres; the Master became a canon of the cathedral, and the members of the confraternity "vassals and knights" of St James the Apostle. Their rule was formally approved by the Pope in 1175. The chaplains of the Order were, probably, canons of the monastery of Santa María de Loyo. The knights were heavily involved in the reconquest of the Iberian Peninsular from Muslims (cf. pp. 132-154), in Portugal as well as Spain – the Portuguese branch becoming more or less autonomous in 1288, and entirely so in 1316. In the fifteenth century the Order became heavily involved in the politics of the Christian kingdoms, and interest in the reconquest declined. It rule of life was unusual because from the first it accepted married members, who took vows of conjugal chastity and were expected to live in the houses of the Order at certain times of the year. During those times, and when the knights were on a campaign, the Order looked after wives and children. In 1493 the Order was annexed to the Crown, a move approved by the pope in 1523. It survived in an honorific capacity until 1835, when all its property was seized, but it still managed to continue to 1931 when it was suppressed by the Spanish government.

Stephen, Order of Saint, founded by Cosimo I de'Medici, and approved by the pope in 1561. Duke Cosimo gave it the name of St Stephen I, pope and martyr, because he had won two important victories on that feast day. The Duke was to be its head, its headquarters were in Pisa, though it naval base – it was primarily intended to defend Italy against attack from the sea by Muslims – was eventually settled at Livorno. The knights had to be of noble

Cosimo I

birth, and were to commit themselves for three years to military service, during which they lived in their convent, under the rule of St Benedict, when not engaged in warfare. The Order did indeed see a fair amount of action (including the battle of Lepanto). It was abolished in 1807 after the invasion of Italy by the French, and though reconstituted in 1817 it was by that time entirely honorific. It was finally abolished in 1859.

Sword Brethren, Order of (Order of Knights of Christ of Livonia), founded 1202 by the Cistercian monk Dietrich, bishop of Estonia. Its base was the city of Riga, and its purpose was the conquest, and conversion, of the pagan tribes of the region, including those of Livonia. In this it was reasonably successful, though it was frequently in conflict with the bishop of Riga over sovereignty of the territories occupied. After a crushing defeat in September 1236 in which very many of the Sword Brethren were killed, the remaining members affiliated with the Teutonic Knights.

Templars (Order of Poor Knights of the Temple of Solomon), founded in Jerusalem c. 1119 by Hugh de Payen, from Champagne. It received its rule at the Council of Troyes in 1128, and from St Bernard of Clairvaux, c. 1135, a treatise *de laude novae militiae*, which in some ways became the charter of the Order, and of subsequent military Orders. Something of its history can be gleaned from this book, (cf. above, chapter 3), and of its demise (cf. above, chapter 8). After the fall of Acre in 1291 its headquarters were moved to Cyprus. At the insistence of Philip II (Philip the Fair) of France it was suppressed by Pope Clement V at the Council of Vienne in 1312. Its last Grand Master was burned at the stake in 1314. In addition to its crusading activities, it acted as banker for many important personages, including popes and the Kings of France and England. Its reputation for great wealth led afterwards to belief in the existence of Templar hidden treasure.

Teutonic Knights (Order of the Hospital of Saint Mary of the Teutons of Jerusalem), founded in 1190, and approved in 1199, as a Hospitaller Order, serving a hospital established by Germans from Bremen and Lübeck, near Acre. In 1198, however, it became a military Order, under the influence of some German crusaders in the Holy Land. In 1230 it was invited by Duke Corrado of Masovia to fight against the pagan Prussians, in return for lordship over the region subjugated. After the fall of Acre the Order moved its headquarters first to Venice and then in 1309 to Marienburg. Two almost independent branches developed, that in Prussia and that in Livonia: the brethren in Livonia from the middle of the fifteenth century elected their own Master. After the pacification of Prussia the Knights found themselves increasingly drawn into conflict with Christian neighbors — especially Poland — and with the discontented population of Prussia. At the battle of Tanneburg in 1410 the Knights were decisively defeated and, in 1457, after a further conflict the Knights lost much of their Prussian territory, had to relocate to Königsberg, and recognize the suzerainty of the King of the Poland. In 1525 the Prussian Grand Master became a Lutheran, and hereditary Duke of Prussia. In 1561 the Grand Master of Livonia also became a Lutheran. Most of the brethren in these two regions conformed to Protestantism, but some in the rest of Germany did not, and the titles of Grand and German Master were combined. In 1696 the Catholic Knights raised a regiment. Though it almost succumbed during the Napoleonic wars, the Order continued until 1923 when for the first time a cleric was elected Grand Master. As a clerical religious Order it still survives.

Teutonic Knight

Thomas of Acre, Order of Saint, founded at Acre in 1192 by King Richard I of England (the Thomas who is the patron saint is Thomas Becket, the martyred Archbishop of Canterbury) as a house of canons caring for the sick. It was transformed into a military Order by Peter des Roches, Bishop of Winchester, in the 1220s. It adopted the rule of the Teutonic Knights, and this received papal confirmation in 1236. It was not a large, and certainly not a wealthy, Order, and it scarcely figures in accounts of battles in the Holy Land. In 1291 its headquarters were moved to Cyprus, but there was a gradual shift of authority to London, which seems to have been more or less complete by the middle of the fourteenth century. This meant the abandonment of any military role, but the Order continued its charitable activities into the sixteenth century, including establishing a school in London. It was dissolved at the Reformation.

Bibliography

The number of books and articles about the crusades in general, and the military Orders in particular, is enormous. Listed below are only those that I have consulted.

Bainton, Roland H., *Christian attitudes toward war and peace* (Nashville TN: Abingdon Press, 1960).

Barber, Malcolm (ed.), *The Military Orders: fighting for the faith and caring for the sick* (Aldershot: Variorum, 1994).

Barber, Malcolm, *The new knighthood: A history of the Order of the Temple* (Cambridge University Press, 1994).

Barber, Richard, *The knight and chivalry* (Woodbridge: The Boydell Press, 1995).

Bernard of Clairvaux, Saint, *Oeuvres completes* vol. 31: 'Éloge de la nouvelle chevalerie' [et al.], introductions, traductions, notes et index par Pierre-Yves Emery (Paris, Cerf, 1990) (Sources chrétiennes 367).

Bhaldraithe, Eoin de, 'Jean Leclerq's attitude toward war', in Elder, E. Rozanne (ed.), *The Joy of Learning and the Love of God* (Kalamazoo: Cistercian Publications, 1995), pp. 217–37.

Bull, Marcus, *Knightly piety and the lay response to the first crusade: The Limousin and Gascony c. 970–1130* (Oxford: The Clarendon Press, 1993).

Burman, Edward, *The Templars, knights of God* (London: Crucible, 1986).

Christiansen, Eric, *The Northern crusades: the Baltic and the Catholic frontier 1100–1525* (London: Macmillan, 1980).

Cowdrey, H. E. J., *Pope Gregory VII, 1073-1085* (Oxford: Clarendon Press, 1998).

Cowdrey, H. E. J., *Popes, monks and crusaders* (London: The Hambledon Press, 1984).

Dawood, N. J. (tr.), *The Koran* (London: Penguin Books, 1974).

Esposito, John (ed.), *The Oxford history of Islam* (Oxford University Press, 1999).

Duncan, Andrew and Opatowski, Michael, *War in the Holy Land from Megiddo to the West Bank* (Stroud: Sutton Publishing, 1998).

Flori, J., 'Guerre sainte et rétributions spirituelles dans la 2e moitié du XIe siecle', *Revue d'Histoire Ecclésiastique* LXXXV (1990), pp. 617–49.

Forey, Alan, *Military Orders and the crusades* (Aldershot: Variorum, 1994).

Forey, Alan, *The military Orders from the twelfth to the early fourteenth centuries* (Basingstoke: Macmillan, 1992).

Fernandez Conde, Javier (ed.), *Historia de la iglesia en Espana, II-1.o: la iglesia en la Espana de los siglos VIII–XIV* (Madrid: Biblioteca de Autores Cristianos, 1983).

Gervers, Michael (ed.), *The second crusade and the Cistercians* (New York: St Martin's Press, 1992).

Guillaume, Alfred, *Islam* (London: Penguin, 1979).

Gutton, Francis, *L'Ordre de Santiago* (Saint Jacques de l' Épée) (Paris: P. Lethielleux, 1972).

Holt, P. M. et al., (eds.), *The Cambridge history of Islam, Vol. I: The Central Islamic Lands* (Cambridge University Press, 1970).

Houseley, Norman, *The later crusades: from Lyons to Alcazar 1274-1580* (Oxford University Press, 1992).

Hunter, David G., 'A decade of research on early Christians and military service',
Religious Studies Review 18 (1992) pp. 87–94.

Johnson, James Turner, *Just war tradition and the restraint of war: a moral and historical inquiry*
(Princeton NJ: Princeton University Press, 1981).

Iogna-Prat, Dominique, *Ordonner et exclure: Cluny et la société chrétienne face a l'hérésie, au judaisme et a l'Islam,
1000–1150* (Paris: Aubier, 2000).

Kedar, Benjamin Z., *Crusade and mission: European approaches toward the Muslims*
(Princeton NJ: Princeton University Press, 1984).

Landes, Richard, *Relics, Apocalypse, and the deceits of history: Ademar of Chabannes, 989–1034*
(Cambridge MA: Harvard University Press, 1993).

Lomax, Derek W. and Mackenzie, David (eds.), *God and man in medieval Spain*
(Warminster: Aris and Phillips, 1989).

Lomax, Derek W., *The reconquest of Spain* (London: Longman, 1978).

Luttrell, Anthony, 'The earliest hospitallers', in Kedar, Benjamin Z. (et al., eds.), *Montjoie: studies in crusade history in
honour of Hans Eberhard Mayer* (Aldershot: Variorum, 1997).

MacKinney, Loren C., 'The people and public opinion in the eleventh-century peace movement',
Speculum V (1930), pp. 181–206.

Maier, Christoph T., *Preaching the crusades: mendicant friars and the cross in the thirteenth century*
(Cambridge University Press, 1994).

Marshall, Christopher, *Warfare in the Latin East, 1192–1291* (Cambridge University Press, 1992).

Mastnak, Toma, *Crusading peace: Christendom, the Muslim world, and western political order*
(Berkeley CA: University of California Press, 2002).

Mulhberger, Steven, 'War, warlords, and Christian historians from the fifth to the seventh century', in Murray,
Alexander Callander (ed.), *After Rome's fall* (Toronto: University of Toronto Press, 1998), pp. 83–98.

Murphy, Thomas Patrick (ed.), *The Holy War* (Columbus OH: Ohio State University Press, 1976).

Nicholson, Helen, *The Knights Templar: A new history* (Stroud: Sutton Publishing, 2001).

Nicholson, Helen (ed.), *The military orders, volume 2: welfare and warfare* (Aldershot: Ashgate, 1998).

Nicholson, Helen, *Templars, Hospitallers and Teutonic Knights: images of the military orders 1128–1291*
(London: Leicester University Press, 1995).

Partner, Peter, *The murdered magicians* (Oxford University Press, 1982).

Peters, F. E., *Jerusalem* (Princeton NJ: Princeton University press, 1985).

Prawer, Joshua, *The world of the crusaders* (London: Weidenfeld and Nicolson, 1972).

Regan, Geoffrey, *The first crusader* (Stroud, Sutton Publishing, 2001)

Riley-Smith, Jonathan (ed.), *The atlas of the crusades* (London: Times Books, 1990).

Riley-Smith, Jonathan, *The first crusade and the idea of crusading* (London: The Athlone Press, 1986).

Riley-Smith, Jonathan (ed.), *The Oxford illustrated history of the crusades* (Oxford University Press, 1995).

Riley-Smith, Jonathan, *What were the crusades?* (London: Macmillan, 1977).

Rocca, Giancarlo (ed.), *Dizionario degli istituti dei perfezione* (Rome: Edizioni Paoline, 1974 –).

Sarnowsky, Jürgen (ed.), *Mendicants, military orders and regionalism in medieval Europe* (Aldershot: Ashgate, 1999).

Seward, Desmond, *The monks of war* (London: Eyre Methuen, 1972).

Sire, H.J.A., *The Knights of Malta* (New Haven and London: Yale University Press, 1994).

Smart, Ninian (ed.), *Atlas of the world's religions* (Oxford University Press, 1999).

Walsh, Michael (ed.), *Dictionary of Christian biography* (London: Continuum, 2001).

Acknowledgements

The books I used are cited in the bibliography. Some were, however, particularly useful. A few I have mentioned in the text, but I would also like to acknowledge how much I depended on Malcolm Barber's *The new knighthood* and Richard Barber's *The knight and chivalry*, on Alan Forey's *The military orders*, Derek Lomax's *The reconquest of Spain*, and on several of the works of Jonathan Riley-Smith. Brendan Smith of the University of Bristol gave me a particularly useful bit of bibliographic advice, and Richard Price of Heythrop College helped me greatly on early Christian attitudes to war. To all these, especial thanks.

Index

A

Abbasids, 45, 47, 49
Abu Talib, 40
Abu Bakr, 35, 42, 133
Acre, 76f, 86, 91, 99, 103ff, 110, 117, 124, 169,
202
Adhemar, bishop of Le Puy, 73
Admiral of the Fleet, Hospitaller, 174
admission, 158f, 161f
Adrian VI, pope, 182
Afonso, King of Portugal, 135f, 138f, 151
Agrippa von Nettesheim, 187f
al-Ahmar, Muhammad ibn Yusuf ibn, 150
Ailly, Pierre de, cardinal, 129f
Aimalric, King of Jerusalem, 94
Aimeric, Duke of Narbonne, 198
Aksum, 39
Alarcos, battle of, 146f
Alaric the Goth, 17
Albanians 175
Albigensians see Cathars
Alcácer do Sal, 149
Alcántara, 142, 148, 193
Alcántara, Order of, 143, 146, 154, 166, 182, 193
Alcobaça, abbey of, 152, 195
Aleppo, 87, 109
Alexander III, pope, 138, 141, 143f
Alexius IV, emperor, 100f
Alexius V, emperor, 101
Alexius Commenus, Emperor, 62, 67, 70, 73, 76
Alfama, castle of, 144, 195
Alfonso I, King of Aragón, 83, 133f, 135
Alfonso II of Aragón, 144
Alfonso VI, King of Castile, 46, 132
Alfonso VII, King of León, 135ff, 137
Alfonso VIII, King of Castile, 142, 146ff
Alfonso IX of Leon, 143, 146, 149
Alfonso X, King of Castile, 153 198
Alfonso XI, of Castile, 151
Alfred, King, 24
Algarve, 136, 149
Algeria 171
Ali, 45, 49, 50f.
Almanzor, 46, 56
Almería, 136
Almizra, Treaty of, 149
Almohads, 136f, 138f, 142, 146, 149
Almoravids, 136
Altopascio, 197
Alvarez, Rodrigo, Count of Sarria, 143f, 200
Amadeus VIII of Savoy, 199
Ambulance Brigade, St John, 185
Americas, conquest of, 183
Amposta, 135
Anatolia, 76, 175
Andalusia, 134, 149

Andrew, King of Hungary, 102, 118
Angevins, 169
Anselm of Lucca, 66
Antioch, 59, 72f., 75, 91, 97, 109f
Antiochus Strategos 21
Antkya see Antioch
Arabia, Christianity in, 37
Aragón, Kingdom of, 132ff, 149, 151, 163, 200
archives, papal, 191
Armenia, 62, 109
Arsuf, 86, 98
Ascalon, 84, 86, 93, 99
Assassins, 94, 109
Athir, Ibn al-, 96
Atlit, 112
Aubrac, Order of, 193
Augustine, St, 82, rule of, 8, 83, 116, 144, 195ff,
199f, on war, 16-18
Austria, 179
Avis, Order of, 152, 157, 181f, 186, 194
al-Azhar Mosque, 50

B

Bacon, Roger, 123
Badajoz, 141
Baghdad, 45, 47
Baghras, 93
Baldwin I, King of Jerusalem,70f, 77
Baldwin IV, King of Jerusalem, 95
Baldwin V, King of Jerusalem, 95
Balearic islands, 149
Balkans, 175
banquet of honor
Barcelona, 137, 149, 199
Barruel, Augustin, 190
Bartolomeo of Vicenzo, 197
Basil, rule of St, 8
Beirut, 86
Belgrade, 175
Benedict, rule of St, 8, 138, 194, 201
Berbers, 49f., 52
Bernard of Clairvaux, St, 79f, 90f, 93, 155
Bethgibelin, 86, 93
Bethlehem, 52
Bethlehem, Order of Our Lady of, 194, 197
Bethlehemites, 194
Beza, battle of, 154
Bible, 52
Black Death, 126
Bodin, Jean, 188
Boethius, 24
Bohemia, 194
Boigny, 169, 198
Bologna, 198
Boniface, General, 17
Bosnians, 175
Brandenburg, Priory of of, 179

Bremen, 202
Britain, 194
Buckland, convent of, 161

C

Cáceres, 139, 141, 201
Caesarea, 8, 86
Cairo, 49, 105, 107, 109f, 176
Calaruega, 115
Calatayud, 133
Calatrava, castle, 135, 137 145, 147, 194
Calatrava La Nueva, castle of, 145, 148
Calatrava, Order of, 137f, 142, 144, 147, 148f, 150,
152ff, 157, 182, 186, 193, 194f, 199f
captives, ransoming, 199
Carrión, 142
Cartagena, 199
Castile, Kingdom of, 133, 135, 146, 149
Castro Marim, 152, 195
Cathars, 113ff, 190, 197
Celestine II, pope, 82
Celestine III, 146
chapters, 166
Charlemagne, 24, 57ff.
Charles Martel, 43
Charles V, Emperor, 176, 187
Charroux, Council of, 30f.
chastity, 166, 201
Christ, Order of, 152, 181, 195
Christian, Bishop, 119, 195
Christians and War, chapter 1 passim, massacre of, 77,
in the Muslim world, 52, 55ff
Cid see El Cid
Cistercians, 9, 79ff, 137f, 141, 157, 160, 165,
167,182, 194ff, 199f, 202
Citeaux, abbey of, 9, 138, 144
Ciudad Real, 195, 200
Ciudad Rodrigo, bishop of, 130
Clairvaux, 80f. see also Bernard of Clairvaux
Clement V, pope, 9, 171ff187, 202
Clement VII, Pope 176
Clerkenwell, 173
Clermont, Council of, 27f., 30, 31, 64, 89
Cluny, abbey of, 8f., 63, 66, 155, 165
Coimbra, 136
Cologne, 187
Columbus, 186
commanderies, 158, 163f, 166, 167
Conrad III, King of Germany, 90, 92
Conrad of Masovia, 118, 120, 202
Conrad of Montferrat, 97, 99
Constance, Council of, 128ff
Constantine, Emperor, 18, 21, 196
Constantinople, 18f., 35f., 42, 68, 87, 89, 192,
capture of by crusaders, 100ff, fall of, 175
Copts, 36
Cordoba, 36, 42, 45f, 136, 150

Cosimo I de'Medici, 201
Council of, see under name of place
Covadonga, battle of, 43
Cracow, University of, 129
Cross, Holy, 23, 96
Crusaders of the Red Star, 194
crusades, 113, first, 69ff, third, 169, peasants',
68ff
Cuarte, battle of, 132
Culmerland, 120
Cyprus, 98f, 112, 169, 171, 192, 196, 202f

D

Damascus, 21, 36, 42, 45, 92f, 103ff, 107f, 109
Danzig, 122
Daroca, castle of, 135, 139
al-Dawla, Sayf, 136
de occulta philosophia 187
de laude novae militiae, 81f, 155
Denmark, 119, 126
dhimmis, 52, 55
Díaz de Bivar, Rodrigo see El Cid
Dietrich, bishop of Estonia, 202
al-Din Zangi, Imad, 87f
al-Din, Nur, 92, 94
Diocletian, Emperor, 15
Dizionario degli Istituti di Perfezione, 193
Dobrin, Order of, see Dobrzyn
Dobrzyn, knights of 119f, 195
Dome of the Rock, 45
Dominic, St, 115, 118
Dominicans, 120 163, 165, 197
Dorylaeum, 70, 91
doweries, 159f
Draper, role of, 165, 167
Dueñas, castle of, 148
Durbe, battle of, 122

E

Ebro, 133, 134, 145
Eco, Umberto, 192
Edessa, 70f, 75,86ff, 92
Edict of Milan, 18
Edward, I, King of England, 150
Edward, prince, 110
Egypt, 49f., 59, 73, 86, 93ff, 99, 104, 106, 171, 174
El Cid, 132f
Eleanor, Infanta of castile, 150
England, 163, 180
Eregli see Herclea
Escaladieu, abbey of, 138
Eskisehir see Dorylaeum
Essenes, 188
Estonia, 119, 122, 126, 202
Estremadura, 149, 201
Étoile, abbey of, 155
Eugenius II, pope, 82
Eugenius III, pope, 89f.

Evora, Order of, 138, 146, 194

F

Faith of Jesus Christ, Order of Knights of the, 197f

Fatima, wife of Alí, 49

Fatimids, 49f., 62, 73, 86

Fénelon, François, 188

Ferdinand II, of Castile, 149f

Ferdinand II, King of Léon, 139, 201

Ferdinand, King of Spain, 154, 186

Fernández, Pedro, 141

"A Field of Blackbirds", 175

Foucault's Pendulum, 192

France, 194

Franciscans, 165

Frederick Barbarossa, Emperor, 98

Frederick II, Emperor, 102ff, 103f, 106, 118, 120

Frederick III, Emperor, 196

Freemasonry, 188-192

French Revolution, 184 190, 194, 198

Fulcher of Chartres, 74f., 76

Fulk, King of Jerusalem, 84

Fustat (Old Cairo), 49

G

Galicia, 135

García, Don, 138

Gaza, 93, 105

Gediminas, Grand Prince of Lithuania, 125

Gelasius II, pope, 133

Gengis Khan, 45

Genoa, 109

George of Alfama, Order of St, 144f, 195, 200

George of Carinthia, Order of St, 196

George of Parma, Order of St, 196

George, patron saint of knights, 125, 150

Geraldo the Fearless, 139f, 141

Gerard, Brother, 83, 85, 196

Germany, 184, 190

Gibraltar, 43, 138

Godfrey of Lower Lotharingia, 75

Godfrey of Bouillon, 79

Gomez, Don, 143

Grail, Holy, 190, 192

Granada, 133, 136, 150.f, 154, 182. 186

Granselve, abbey of, 153, 199

Gregory VII, pope, 63ff.

Gregory VIII, pope, 97

Gregory IX, pope, 102

Guibert of Nogent, 66

Guy de Lusignan, King of Jerusalem, 95f, 99

Guy de Ridefort, Master of the Temple, 95

H

Hagia Sophia, church of, 101

Haifa, 86

al-Hakim, 59ff.

Hamah, Sultan of, 105

Hammer-Purgstall, Joseph, 190

Harbiyah see La Forbie

Hartwig II, Bishop of Bremen, 118

Helena, Empress, 21

Henry III, King of England, 168

Henry IV, King of England, 125

Henry IV, King of France, 198

Henry IV, King of German, 66

Henry the Navigator, 181

Heraclius, Emperor, 22f

Herclea, 70

Hippolytus, canons of, 15f.

Holland, 180

Holy Sepulchre, canons of, 134, 189

Holy Sepulchre, church of, 60, 62f., 68, 75, 83f.

Holy Sepulchre, Order of, 175

Honorius III, pope, 102

Horns of Hattin, battle of, 96ff, 146

Hospitallers, 7, 10, 13, 24, 63-112 passim, 117, 134, 137, 142f, 144, 148, 152, 154f, 169, 171, 173-79 184, 192f, 195f, 197f fleet 171, 174, 184, rule 157-68 passim

Hugh, bishop of Jabala, 89

Hugh of St Victor, 81

Hugh of Champagne, count, 80

Hugh de Payen, 77ff., 81ff. 155, 202

Humbert of Romans, 163

Hungary, 175, 179

Hus, Jan, 129

I

Iconium, 70

indulgences, 89

Innocent II, pope, 99f, 102

Innocent III, pope, 113ff, 119, 123, 138, 147 159

Innocent VIII, pope, 198

Isaac of Stella 155

Isabella, Queen of Castile, 154, 186

Isidro, Saint, 148

Islam, see chapter 2 passim, and war, 40ff, see also Ismailis, Kharijites, Shi'ites, Sunnis, Muslims

Ismailis, 51f.

Istanbul, 19

Italy, 137, 194, 201

Ivanhoe, 191

Iznik, see Nicaea

J

Jacinto, 141, 146 see also Celestine III

Jacobites, 188, Christian Church, 26

Jadwiga, Queen of Poland, 126

Jaén, Treaty of, 150

Jaffa, 77, 103, 103

James of Altopascio, Order of St, 197

James of the Sword, Order of, 182

James, Saint, 150, 201

janissaries, 192

Jaume I, of Aragón, 149, 151

Jaume II, of Aragón, 153

Jerez, 150

Jerusalem, 21, 37, 42, 45, 54f., 107, 144, 196, 198, 200, 202, battle for, 73ff, kingdom of, 75, King of, 87, fall of to Saladin, 97, attempted liberation of, 98f, pilgrimage to, 60, 77, 83, 89, 200

Jerusalem, Patriarch of, see Patriarch of Jerusalem

Jesuits 190, 196

Jesus Christ, Order of, 197, see also Faith of Jesus Christ

Jews, 172, in the Muslim world, 52, 55, treatment by crusaders, 68, 86, massacre of, 74

Jogailo, Grand Prince of Lithuania, 126f, 129ff

John VIII, pope, 66

John XXIII, (anti)pope, 128f

John of Austria, 182

John of Brienne, King of Jerusalem, 103

John of Damascus, Saint, 36, 47

John of Falkenberg, 130

John of Jerusalem, Order of St, see Hopsitallers

John of Tour, 172

John the Baptist, St, 188

John, Venerable Order of St, 185

Jordan, River, 86

Julian, Emperor, 20

Julián de Pereiro, Order of, 143, 193

K

Karlowitz, Treaty of, 179

Kerbogha, Atabeg of Mosul, 72

Kharijites, 51

Khorezmian Turks, 107

Khusrau, 20ff..

knighthood, 24ff.157, 159

Knighthood of Christ in Livonia see Sword Brethren

Knights of Dobrzyn see Dobrzyn, Knights of

Könisberg, 181, 203

Konya see Iconium

Kosovo, 175

Krac de Chevaliers, 84

L

La Coruña, 199

La Forbie, battle of, 107

Lance, Holy, 73

langues,167, 173, 185

Las Navas de Tolosa, battle of, 148

Lateran Council, 102, 144, 159

Latvia see Livonia

Lazarus, Order of St, 85, 111, 169, 175, 185,188, 194, 197f

Lemnos, 194

Leo IV, Pope, 50, 66

León, Kingdom of, 135, 142, 146, 193

León-Castile, Kingdom of, 151

Lepanto, battle of 178, 182, 201

Licinius, Emperor, 18

Limassol, 107

Lisbon, 42 149

literacy 157f

Lithuania, 122f., 125, 126

Livonia, 118, 120, 179, 181, 202f, see also Teutonic Knights

Livorno, 201

Lobo, king, 136, 138

Loderengo Andalb, 198

Loja, battle of, 154

London, 82, 168, 171, 173, 188, 203, University of, 191

Louis VII, King of France, 90, 92

Louis IX, King of France, 107f, 168

Louis XIV, King of France, 188

Lübeck, 202

Lucca, 197

Lucena, battle of, 133

Lusignans, 169

Luther, Martin, 181

M

Macedonia 175

Madrid, 148

Mahdi, 51

Málaga, 133, 136

Mallén, lordship of, 135

Malta, 176-79, 184, 196f

Malta, Knights of, see Hospitallers

Mamluks, 49, 110ff, 174ff

al-Mansur, Caliph, 47

al-Mansur, Abu Amir, see Almanzor

Mansurah, 107

Manuel, Emperor, 91

Manzikert, battle of, 62 65, 68

Maras see Marash

Marash, 70

Marcus Aurelius, 14

Maria de Espaa, Santa, Order of, 153

Marienberg, castle of, 125, 127, 180

Maronites, 36

Marshal, role of, 167

Mary of Spain, Order of, 198f

Mary of the Latins, Abbey of St, 83

Mary, Order of, 198

Masonry see Freemasonry

Master, role of, 166f

Matilda, countess, 197

Maurice, Emperor, 20f.

Maurice, Order of St, 198f

Maxmilian, martyr, 14f.

Mecca, 37ff, 48, 49f.

Medina, 40ff., 45, 48, 49

Melikites, 36

Mémoires pour servier l'histoire du Jacobinisme, 190

Mercedarians, 199

Metternich, Prince Klemens von, 190

Michael VII Ducas, Emperor, 65

Michelet, Jean, 191

Milan, Edict of, 18

Milstatt, castle of, 196

Moclin, battle of, 151, 153, 199

Mohacs, battle of, 176

Moissac, abbey of, 64

Molay, Jacques de, 171ff, 187, 189, 191

Mongols, 45, 109f, 121

Monte Gaudio, Order of, 143f, 200

Montesa, Order of, 152, 154, 182, 186, 196, 199f

Montfort, castle of, 117, 124

Montfragüe, 200

Montmorillon, Order of, 200

Morimond, abbey of, 138, 152, 153, 194f

Morocco, 136

Mosul, 72, 87

Mount Carmel, Our Lady of, 198

Mozarabs, 46

Mu'awiya, 51

Muhammad, 35f., 37ff., 48, 190

Murcia, 149, 151

Muslims, see chapter 2, passim, 129, 186,199, 201,
        massacre of, 74, 110 see also Islam

al-Mutasim, caliph, 49

Mutawakkil, Caliph, 55

Mystery of Baphomet Revealed, 190

N

Nablus, Council of, 77

Napoleon, 184, 191, 197, 203

Narbonne, 198, battle of, 43, Council of, 32, 34

Navarre, 146, 147

Nestorians 36

Nevsky, Alexander, 121

Nicaea, 69, 70, 73

Nicholas IV, pope 171

Nile, River, 107

Normans, 70

Novgorod, 121, 125, 129, 131

novitiate, 157, 161

Nubia, 50

nuns, 160f

Nusayr, Musa bin, 42, 45

O

office, divine, 158, 163

Old Man of the Mountains, 94, 108

Origen, 14

Orleans, 198

Osma, 115

Ottomans, 175, 179, 184

P

Paris, 168, 172f, 188, 191 University of, 129

Parma, 196

Partner, Peter, 187

Paschal II, pope, 76

Patriarch of Constantinople, 22

Patriarch of Jerusalem, 21f., 52, 93, 102, 104, 191

Paul I, Tsar of Russia, 185

Paul II, pope, 196

peace of God see truce of God

Pedro II, King of Aragon, 144

Peipus, Battle of Lake, 121

Pelagius, cardinal, 103

Pelayo, 43

Pepin, 43

Peter I, King of Aragón, 195

Peter the Venerable, abbot 155

Peter Nolasco, 199

Peter des Roches, 203

Peter the Hermit, 68, 70

Philip II, King of France, 98, 172ff, 187, 202

Philip II, King of Spain, 182

Piacenza, Council of, 67

pilgrimage, 193, to Jerusalem see Jerusalem

pilgrimage, to Compostella see Santiago

Pisa, 201, Council of, 128

Pius II, Pope, 194

Poland, 126f, 175 180f, 202f

Portugal, Kingdom of, 135, 146, 183, 193f

poverty, 165

preceptories, see commanderies

priests, 160

priories see provinces

provinces, 166

Prussia, 202, see also Teutonic Knights

Pskov, 121, 125, 129, 131

Puerto de Santa Maria, 199

Q

Qu'ran, 38, 50, 52, 56, 62, 155

Quantum praedecessores, 89f. 113

R

al-Rahman, Abd, 45

Ramon Lull, 171

Ramsay, (Chevalier) Andrew Michael, 188f

al-Rashid, Harun, 5 7

Raymond VI, count of Toulouse, 113, 198

Raymond, abbot of Fitero, 137f, 194

Raymond, count of Tripoli, 95f.

Raymond du Puys, Master of the Hospital, 83f

Raymond-Roger, viscount of Béziers, 113

Red Sea, 50

Reisen, 125

responsions, 161, 174

Rhodes 167, 171, 173f, 178, 185, siege of 175f.,
        196f

Ricardo Filiangieri, 105f.

Richard I, King of England, 13, 97f., 169, 192 203

Richard of Cornwall, 106

Riga, 123, 126, 202

Robert of Flanders, 67

Rodez, 193

Roland see *Song of Roland*

Romanus Diogenes, Emperor, 65

Rome, 50, 63, 185, 197

Roncesvalles, 58

Rossetti, Dante Gabriele, 191

Rossetti, Gabriele, 190f

S

Sa'ad ibn Mardanish, Muhammad ibn, see Lobo

Safad, castle of, 105

saints, 165

Saladin, 95ff, 98f.

Salamanca, University of, 150

Samarra, 49

Samogitians, Lithuanian tribe, 127, 131

San Sebastián, 199

Sancho II, King of Castile, 132, 137

Santa Creus, abbey of, 152, 200

Santiago de Compostella, 141f, 193, 197

Santiago Matamoros, 150

Santiago, Order of, 141ff, 146, 151, 147, 149,
        152ff , 157, 159, 165, 174, 178 182, 186,
        199, 201

Saracens, 52, see also Muslims

Sarría, 200

Savoy, House of, 199

scholarship, Arab, 47

Schoten, battle of, 122

Scotland, 194

Scott, Sir Walter, 191f

Selim the Grim, 176

Seljuk Turks, 60f, 65, 70, 76.

Seneschal, 167

Serbs, 175

sergeants, 161f

Sergius IV, pope, false letter of, 64f.

Sergius, Patriarch of Constantinople, 22

Seville, 133, 150

Shapur I, 19f.

Shapur II, 20

Shi'ites, 51

Sidon, 86, 111

Sigena, convent of, 160

Sigismund, Emperor, 128

Simon de Montfort, 113f

Smith, Admiral Sir Sydney, 192

Sobieski, John, King of Poland, 179

Solomon, 188, 202

Song of Roland, 57f.

Spain, 56, 132-154 passim, 183

Spanish Civil War, 200

Springs of Cresson, battle of, 95

St Andrews, University of, 194

Stephen, Order of St, 197, 201

Suleyman the Magnificent, 176, 197

Sunnis, 50f.

Switzerland, 184

Sword Brethren 118ff, 122f, 202

T

Tagus, River, 142, 145

Tannenberg, battle of, 127, 203

Tarifa, battle of, 151

Tarik, 42f., 45, 46

Tarragona, 89, 195

Tashfins, Yusuf ibn, 59

Templar Marshal, 108

Templars, 7, 9, 10, 24, 63-112 passim, 117, 134f,
        137, 139, 142, 144, 147, 154, 169, 174, 185,
        188, 195, 200, 202, banking system, 110,
        167f, criticism of 155f, myth 187-192, rule
        156-68 passim, suppression, 152, 172f

Temple 188, 202, Mount, 73

Tertullian, 13

Teruel, 144

Teutonic Knights, 7, 84f. 104, 109ff, 117-131
        passim, 145, 179, 185, 195f, 202f, rule of,
        156-68 passim

The Talisman, 191

Theodosius, Emperor, 16f.

Thomas of Acre, Order of, 85, 111, 167, 169, 171,
        185, 203

Thomas Aquinas, 130, 156, 183, on war 115ff

Thorn, castle of, 120

Thorn, Second Treaty of, 180

Thorn, Treaty of, 127

Tiberias, Lake of, 96

Toledo, 42, 46, 57, 137, 142, 146f

Tomar, castle of, 152, 195

Tortosa, 145, 195

Toulouse, 198, battle of, 43, Council of, 133,
        siege of, 115

tournaments, 26

Transjordan, 86

Transylvania, 179

Trent, Council of, 199

Treviso, 198

Tripoli, 75, 87, 97

Troyes, Council of, 77f, 81, 156, 202

truce of God, 29f., 32, 67, 130

Trujillo, 139

Tunis, 110

Turin, Shroud of, 192

Turks, 49, 59, 91, 174, 178, 181, see also Seljuks,
        Mamluks, Ottomans, Khorezmian

Twelvers, 51

Tyre, 75, 86, 97, 105

U

Ubayd Allah, 49

Umar, 42, 45, 52, 54

Umayyads, 45f.

United States, 190

Urban II, pope, 63ff, 67ff, 69, 72, 75, 89,

Urban III, pope, 97

Urfa see Edessa

usury. 168

Uthman, 45, 47, 50

V

Valencia, 132f, 149, 182, 199

Valetta, 178

Valette, Jean de, 176f

Van, Lake, 62

Velázquez, Diego, 137

Venice, 99ff, 109, 123, 169, 178, 202

Vezelay, 90, 98

Vienna, 179

Vienne, Council of, 202

Villaret, Foulques de, 171

Vistula, River, 195

Vitoria, Francsico de, 130, 182

Vladimiri, Peter, 129f

W

Walter of Mesnil, 94

war, and Christians, see chapter 1 passim, Vitoria on,
        183f, and Islam, 40ff

Wends, crusade against, 93

William the Conqueror 32

William of Tyre, 60f., 74, 77

Wilson, Ian, 192

Witwold, Grand Prince of the Samogitians, 127, 129,
        131

Wladyslaw see Jogailo

Wycliffe, John, 129

Y

Yathrib see Medina

Yemen, 50

Z

Zaragossa, 57. 132f

Zoroastrians, 37